BASEBALL'S

ALL · TIME

DREAM

TEAM

JOHN P. McCARTHY, JR.

BASEBALL'S
ALL ○ TIME
DREAM TEAM

JOHN P. McCARTHY, Jr.

B

BETTERWAY BOOKS
CINCINNATI, OHIO

Photos courtesy of the National Baseball Library and Archive, Cooperstown, New York.

Baseball's All-Time Dream Team. Copyright © 1994 by John P. McCarthy. Printed and bound in the United States of America. All rights reserved. No part of this book may be reproduced in any form or by any electronic or mechanical means including information storage and retrieval systems without permission in writing from the publisher, except by a reviewer, who may quote brief passages in a review. Published by Betterway Books, an imprint of F&W Publications, Inc., 1507 Dana Avenue, Cincinnati, Ohio 45207. 1-800-289-0963. First edition.

98 97 96 95 94   5 4 3 2 1

Library of Congress Cataloging in Publication Data

McCarthy, John P.
  Baseball's all time dream team / by John P. McCarthy.
      p.   cm.
  Includes bibliographical references and index.
  ISBN 1-55870-329-2
  1. Baseball players—United States—Biography. 2. Baseball players—United States-Statistics. 3. Baseball players—United States—Ratings of.
  I. Title.
GV865.A1M37 1994
796.357'092'2—dc20   93-35612
[B]   CIP

Edited by Thomas Clark
Interior design by Paul Neff
Cover design by Paul Neff
Cover illstration by Paul Neff

PART ONE

The Approach to the All-Time Dream Team

Offense, Defense and Opinion

Chapter One

Baseball's Dream Team: Why? How? Key Issues

O K, why did I write this book? Why such a fuss? Why do fans argue about who were the greatest baseball players of all time? I guess sociologists can write textbooks discussing such questions, but it's all quite simple to me. Baseball is an American passion. We love our game of bats and balls, and we honor it and its heroes by remembering them.

It's just a game? Well, tell that to a nine-year-old standing wobbly-knee'd in the batter's box, butterflies fluttering in his stomach, feeling like he is about to do the only important thing in all of life — both thrilled by and dreading the moment.

Passion? I remember as a young boy watching games on TV. I must have been in about fourth grade. Whenever a great player like Willie Mays came up to the plate, I had this little ritual. I would place cushions from the couch along the floor leading up to the TV. Then I would stand on the couch, and just as the pitcher went into his delivery, I would leap toward the TV, bounding from cushion to cushion, doing a somersault at the end. Landing on my feet, I'd let out a war cry right at the TV screen. I was absolutely convinced that if I timed it perfectly, a home run would be hit.

It wasn't that I was such a good player myself. Like many kids, I struggled in Little League. My friends and I played ball endlessly in nearby hay fields, but I was growing so fast that the "eye-hand" connections were all jumbled.

In any event, one spring day in about seventh grade, we went out to hit some balls. We hadn't played all winter and were eager to get in a few licks. But when I hit the first pitch, something incredible happened. The ball soared way out into the sky, for what seemed like a mile. I'll never forget that moment. A power hitter had suddenly emerged from the "ugly duckling." It was a rite of passage. After that, I kept playing ball until well past forty years of age, and coached Little League for eighteen years.

I'm not sure if that answers why I wrote this book, but it explains it fully to me.

I began this book with great enthusiasm. The very thought of freely roaming throughout baseball's history to closely review its heroes renewed my boyhood fascination with America's national pastime. I saw in baseball's infancy a gentleman's game with underhand pitching and mitten gloves. Then came the youthful period of spitballs, slapstick hitting and grizzly tough ballplayers. Fans came to games in formal dress. A truly Golden Age finally blossomed when mighty sluggers squared up against exploding fastballers and lifted thunderous clouts to the very clouds above.

But, after many months of agonizing over subtle differences, I have learned that comparing the greatest ballplayers is tough. It's hard enough with players I have personally followed over the years. I remember as a young boy the endless debates between my dad and uncles about whether Willie Mays or Mickey Mantle was the better player. An occasional Dodger fan would offer the name Duke Snider and would be roundly chastised! How then do we judge players whom none of us have ever seen? Or those who played in distinct eras with oceans of difference between them?

Actually, I had started to put together my own dream team a few years ago, just for the fun of it. I read a few books that made their own attempts, but I found all fell short of the mark. Many relied too much on mere opinion. The 1992 *Sports Illustrated* dream team is one example that was severely criticized. At other times, I found an overreliance on single-faceted statistics like the batting average, which is clearly inadequate to measure the full offensive impact of hitters. Other "teams" engaged in a casual or inconsistent use of certain statistics, or, worst of all, fashioned contrived statistics or estimates that were complex and too hard to understand. Some all-time selections ignored defense completely, and I have learned why. Finding the appropriate balance between hitting and fielding may be the toughest call of all.

FACTS OR FANCY?

What about statistics? These are the time-honored measures of a player's performance. The good thing about numbers is that they are objective. They don't lie; they don't bend to emotions; and they don't forget greatness after the passage of time. Yet we must use numbers wisely. To that end, I'll present in the next chapter a single statistic that captures all the different aspects of being a good batter: power, baserunning, walks and hits. I'll also suggest some ways to compare ballplayers from the different periods of baseball. My point is that statistics, such as batting averages, are pretty much always counted the same, so they are important, objective evidence of who are the best hitters ever.

The problem with numbers is that they only say what they say. No matter how much we jam into a statistic, it can never capture the whole player. This is particularly true for defense where the available statistics are woefully inadequate. Furthermore, no statistic can measure something like leadership, or field generalship, or the other intangibles that make some players sure "winners." Numbers can't convey the electrifying impact of certain players, or their ability to lift a whole team or a whole stadium of fans. So we also need to consider opinions, informed opinions, of those who regularly watched the game and saw the players perform, those who were close enough and knowledgeable enough to identify the best of all.

Of course, anyone who loves the game will invariably begin to form emotional attachments to certain players. And this is the big problem with opinions. People will tend to favor players from their own time, those they saw the most. Some of the purported greatness of certain players seems to arise from a mythology which has grown around them, perhaps created and sustained by the media. These myths add to the perception of their greatness, forming an insurmountable barrier for a newer and better player to overcome. We must have the courage to debunk myths when evident, but at the same time we must honor the ability of the legend to capture qualities of true greatness.

So, I will respect both fact and fancy, and search for the appropriate balance between statistics and opinions. This is a key difference between this book and others' attempts.

In striking that balance between the numbers and the opinions, I will tend to favor the numbers, since I think we have developed some excellent statistics, particularly for measuring offense. I also think we need to give a bit more weight to the numbers because no one has seen every ballplayer over baseball's hundred-plus year official history. But when things get close, and they will get awfully close, we need to hear from the fans, the writers, the players and the coaches.

GOOD FIELD, NO HIT?
The next big issue then is how much weight to give to hitting and how much to defense. The modern statistical wizards have developed formulas to suggest that great batters will single-handedly win eighty to ninety games with their bats during their careers, while the great defensemen (infielders) will win only twenty to twenty-five with their gloves. The wizards maintain that a great hitter will generate nearly ten times as

Mickey Cochrane makes the tag at home plate.

many runs as a great fielder will save. In the infield, where defense is more important, the ratio is much smaller, but the number men still claim it's better than two to one in favor of offense. I frankly don't have much faith in the complex defensive formulas, but they make a stunning point.

On the other hand, a funny thing happens when you look at opinion polls. We will go into this in more detail later, but the great defensemen are often rated much more highly than the formulas would suggest, even if their hitting was merely average. This pattern was true not just in the old days, but continues in more recent surveys.

Surely, great defensive play is a beautiful thing to behold. Since the opinion polls pretty clearly contradict the number crunchers as to its value, this suggests to us that there is a bit more to baseball than just scoring runs, at least to the fans.

Still, the plain truth is that defensive gems just don't occur that often. A player fields only a few chances per game, and most plays are fairly routine. But, an at bat is *always* a chance to score.

Basically, my approach is to give much more weight to hitting for the power positions (outfield, first base), and to rate defense more equally for the fielding positions (second base, shortstop). Catchers and third base fall in between. Both hitting and fielding are always important, but it's a matter of emphasis. My approach for outfield is to first identify the great hitters, and *then* to see who could also catch. For infield, I first require great fielding ability, and then see which of the great fielders could also hit.

I also have loosely imposed a Hall of Fame requirement. I decided early that a player must be in the Hall of Fame (unless he is an active player, or not yet eligible for the Hall) in order to make the dream team. Of course, I evaluate some who aren't there, but it turns out that there are few players not in the Hall who could seriously contend for the Dream Team. Guys like Nellie Fox, Marty Marion, Billy Williams, Phil Rizzuto and Dick Allen, as well as a slew of old timers like Harry Stovey and Ross Barnes, should be in the Hall, but no one would seriously contend they are the "all-time best" at their positions.

THE FLASH IN THE PAN

There is a genre of current literature that looks at how good players were in their peak years, as opposed to their overall career performance. Sometimes these discussions discount the poorer statistics usually found at the end of the careers of players such as a Willie Mays or a Hank Aaron, who significantly lowered their lifetime stats in their last five years. Then there were players with great promise who got injured or died young. "Lady" Baldwin won forty-two games in 1886, but blew his arm pitching those 487 innings. Addie Joss played only eight years, compiling an 1.88 ERA, second lowest ever, but died of meningitis. Mickey Mantle and Sandy Koufax had a few of the best years ever played in the game, but did not sustain performance for twenty-plus years like a Willie Mays, a Ty Cobb or a Cy Young.

I believe most sports fans favor career statistics as the best measure of the greatest. A lot of players may have had some exceptional years, but the greatest are those who did it year in and year out. Thus, my approach here will be to evaluate players primarily in terms of lifetime performance. I will consider peak performance in close cases, but I will give the benefit of a doubt to those who maintained excellence for the long run.

The following chapters will present general information in three areas: the offensive hitting statistics, the defensive fielding statistics and, finally, the opinions and perceptions that have been reported in polls, surveys and written literature over the years on who was the best. I will rank and rate the best player in each category. After presenting these findings, we move into Part Two, where I analyze it all, position by position, and select the dream team.

Chapter Two

The Greatest Hitters

The road to the All-Time Dream Team in baseball starts with hitting. It's the essence of the game, its heart, its soul, and its joy!

I coached Little League for nearly twenty years, and much of that experience was covered in my first book, *A Parent's Guide to Coaching Baseball*. I always started off the new season with two messages. First, I told the players that they were all hitters, and repeated it until they believed it. Second, I taught them to listen for the sound of a well-hit ball. It has a distinctive crack, a powerful and penetrating sound in a close game. It signifies that real baseball contact has been made. Kids learned to listen for that sound. We shouted when we heard it in practice. Eventually, kids tried to cause that sound themselves, and hitters emerged!

Baseball is America's all-time favorite sport, and the heart of the game is hitting. Sure, great pitching will usually dominate a game, and defense wins close pennant races, but hitting is the element that brings us to the game! An old-timer once told me that "Defense is something you do while you're waiting to hit!"

Anyone who has ever hit, or seen a loved one hit, a home run knows exactly what I mean. For a solitary moment everyone is breathless, watching the ball shudder as it fights against the wind currents. As it floats down, all eyes strain to see if it will clear the outfield fence, and a moment of awe and disbelief is shattered by a roar erupting from deep within the crowd. So, the honor of being the best hitter, or even among the best hitters ever, is simply beyond my imagination. Hitting is where we start!

THE HOLY GRAIL: THE SEARCH FOR AN ULTIMATE BATTING STATISTIC

I'm going to make a statement here which I will develop as I go on. It is a key to building an All-Time Dream Team. What we need is *a single understandable offensive statistic that includes all key aspects of batting and works over all of baseball's history.*

We simply don't have one. The batting and slugging averages leave out such aspects as walks and steals. In addition, the complicated formulas of the modern wizards are not understandable to the average fan and do not work over all of baseball's history.

There are numerous books honoring the great hitters of the past, but none convincingly demonstrate which hitters were The Best. We are bombarded with showers of numbers, batting averages, slugging percentages, on-base percentages, net steals and walk/strikeout ratios. But we don't have a single, easily understandable statistic that includes all of these. Not that one number should ever settle the debate; such a number cannot be devised. But we need a number that includes all aspects of batting performance, so we can all start on the same page when comparing players.

Our ultimate statistic must also allow us to judge players from even the earliest eras. Many writers, when comparing hitters from the different eras of baseball, entirely ignore the period prior to 1900, almost as if it never existed.

Sure, there were great differences in the game in the very old days. Prior to 1893 the pitcher was only forty-five to fifty feet from the batter. Old Hoss Radbourn used to bounce the ball in front of the plate so it would rise up into the strike zone. Walks were awarded only after nine balls, slowly decreasing to four balls over a ten-year period. The strike zone began well over the batter's head, and later bounced back and forth a few times between the armpit and top of the shoulders. Today it's quite small, just above the waist. At one point strikes did not even exist, and bats could be flat on one side. A stolen base was awarded if the runner went from first to third on a single. Prior to 1884 pitching was underhanded, similar to fast-pitch softball (try it if you think it's easy!). In baseball's formative years, from 1839 to 1860, the pitches were all slow, and the batter would signal exactly where he wanted the ball.

Think about it. It's the way we played as kids. Put the ball over the plate and let him hit it. This game was originally about hitting, not pitching.

By 1871, however, professional ball was well established with the formation of the National League, and formal statistics were recorded. The game was in its infancy, but there were great athletes on the diamond, such as Buck Ewing, Ed Delahanty, Bill Hamilton and Dan Brouthers, and these pioneers of the game deserve our continuing respect.

By the turn of the century, during the era of the "dead ball," baseball was a game of singles, speed and baserunning skills. We are so accustomed to our modern slugging style of play that we sadly underestimate the ability of the great place hitters such as Ty Cobb and Nap Lajoie, who used their superb talents to find a way to slap the dull, sometimes lopsided, ball into defensive gaps, and then turned to great baserunning skills to terrorize defenses.

The more lively ball was introduced just before the Roaring Twenties, and the slugfest of the Golden Age of baseball began, lasting into the 1960s, interrupted only by the Second World War. Babe Ruth, Lou Gehrig, Ted Williams and Willie Mays were a few of the many great players of this era.

How do we compare these players to each other? Not that there can ever be an exact formula, and not that *numero uno* is necessarily so much better than number ten on the list. But it *is* a game, and people want to compare. In this chapter, I will suggest a way to compare players seventy years apart. It's a fairly simple concept.

Less difficult is the problem of comparing players of the same time period who had very different statistics. Wade Boggs hit a lot of singles for the highest career average (.338) of the recent past, but how do we compare him to Mike Schmidt, who hit at only a .270 pace but belted 530 home runs? Again I will offer a relatively simple way to compare the offensive performance of these players, by presenting a statistic which incorporates all aspects of offensive play: hitting, power hitting, baserunning and walks.

None of this would be possible without the enormous effort of those baseball nuts who have spent countless hours scouring old records for players' lifetime stats. Special appreciation is given to a real pioneer, Henry Chadwick, who was the first to report baseball averages in 1865; to Joseph L. Reichler for *The Baseball Encyclopedia*; to David S. Neft, Roland T. Johnson, Richard M. Cohen and Jordan A. Deutsch for *The Sports Encyclopedia: Baseball*; to Mike Shatzkin for *The Ballplayers*; and most especially to John Thorn and Pete Palmer for *Total Baseball*, a book that has been by my side for many months. Many of these people and others are part of a group known as The Society for American Baseball Research (SABR), and have introduced a new, albeit sometimes complicated, approach to statistics often referred to as *sabermetrics*. This book would simply not be possible but for their great efforts to reveal the facts.

THE EARNED BASES AVERAGE

When a hitter steps to the plate, his job is to get on base and to grab as many bases as possible. Once he gets on, it's pretty much up to someone else to move him along. Sure, it would be nice to knock in a few runs, since that's what wins games, but someone has to be on base for that to happen. *The only thing the hitter can control by himself is his initial act of hitting and baserunning. A player can earn bases.* So, that's what we need to measure.

A hitter can get a single, a double, a triple, a home run or a walk. A double earns two bases, and should therefore count twice what a single does, and so forth. Yet, the batting average lumps all hits together. A home run and a single are just "hits," perhaps because it's simpler to count them all equally, perhaps because singles were about all a batter could get during the "dead ball" era of 1880-1919 when the batting average was first devised. Anyway, the traditional "batting average" of hits divided by at bats was the main measure of batting prowess, and is still the primary statistic used today. It certainly has the virtue of simplicity, and is easy to understand. It's so easy to just count hits!

However, most fans understand that this statistic is quite limited as a measure of a hitter's true contribution to the game. Bases on balls are not figured into the batting average, even as an at bat! A *walk* was viewed in the old days with even less regard than it is today, and walks were not easily awarded under early rules. However, "a walk is as good as a hit" is a familiar adage today, and any knowledgeable fan knows that walks turn into runs. It is simple blindness to ignore walks when measuring offensive production.

After the livelier ball was introduced, multiple base hits became more common to the game, so the concept of a slugging average emerged. This statistic counts doubles, triples and homers and tallies their respective base totals. It basically counts the number of bases earned with each hit, and divides by the number of at bats. Yet it does not take the logical, next step of including walks and net stolen bases as I believe the *ultimate statistic* must. After all a single and a stolen base are just about as good as a double, right? Well, not quite. Stolen bases can't generate RBIs, so they are slightly less valuable, but not enough to require us to get involved in complex fractions.

In pursuit of an ultimate statistical measure, the number wizards of SABR have calculated the precise value of a home run as compared to a single, and so forth. It turns out, they claim, that a homer is not really as valuable as four singles in

Ty Cobb beats a throw to the bag.

generating runs. The actual value is more like 3.15. A triple is 2.2 times as good as a single, a double is 1.7 times as valuable, a walk is about three-quarters as good, and a steal is a bit under half (.42) as good. (These are modern day values, remember, and do not reflect the values of the early dead-ball days when baserunning was much more important to winning.)

As neat as these numbers appear to be, I believe that the value of a baseball game is more than just runs and winning. Winning is the players' aim, but there is also a transcendent beauty to great hits. It is that beauty that puts fans into the seats and visions of grandeur into kids' fantasies. A homer can immeasurably lift the spirits of a team, or take the wind out of opponents. So I challenge a mathematical construct which devalues the extra bases earned by sluggers or speedsters. (Besides, it is hard enough to get tradition to move away from mere batting averages, and we'll never do it if we think the average fan is going to understand a concept such as the *linear weights* formula of the sabermetricians.) I may take issue with the details of this important work, but I will include their sabermetrics in my charts and be influenced by their numbers as I fill out my dream team lineup. I just part company with using "estimates" of runs generated as a primary measure of who was the best ever.

Instead, we will use this easy calculation:

Earned Base Average =

$$\frac{\text{Singles} + 2 \times \text{Doubles} + 3 \times \text{Triples} + 4 \times \text{Homers} + \text{Walks} + \text{Net Steals}}{\text{\# of Plate Appearances}}$$

The term *plate appearances* reminds us that we add at bats plus walks in the denominator. Complicated? Not at all! It just counts the number of bases earned for each time a player comes to bat. That's why I call this statistic the *earned bases average* or *EBA*. It allows us to compare the value of the singles, doubles and steals of the Ty Cobbs with the homers of the Ruths, Mantles and Mayses. In effect, it combines the essence of the batting average, the slugging average and the on-base percentage.

Let's do a "for instance." We'll use Babe Ruth.

The Babe had:	1,517 singles	× 1 =	1,517
	506 doubles	× 2 =	1,012
	136 triples	× 3 =	408
	714 homers	× 4 =	2,856
	2,056 walks	× 1 =	2,056
	123 steals	× 1 =	123
	Total bases		**7,972**
	Minus 118 times caught stealing		-118
	Total bases earned		**7,854**

His plate appearances include:	at bats	8,399
	plus walks	2,056
	Total plate appearances	**10,455**

So, The Babe's **Earned Bases Average** is: 7,854/10,455 = .751

I am certainly not the first to suggest an "ultimate" statistic. In his superb "must read" *Baseball Abstract*, Bill James, an Einstein of baseball numerology, proposes a similar statistic, which he proves is highly related to generating runs. The statistic is basically the earned bases average multiplied by the number of successful plate appearances. It makes sense that if you multiply the number of bases per appearance by the number of successful appearances, you will approximate the number of runs generated. I don't feel the need to multiply EBA by successful at bats, since it merely converts earned bases into estimated runs. It is an unnecessary step. Estimated runs just complicates the matter. James needed about fifteen versions of his formula to adjust for the absence of certain data in certain decades and, more important, to adjust for the transition from speed and base stealing of the early days to the modern slugging game.

Now, I am pretty comfortable with mathematics and even with most high-powered statistics, but I had to struggle to understand these formulas. I assume that those who don't deal with stats regularly are lost with much of the stuff around now. My EBA is simple, works well for each baseball era, and is the best single statistic for the job. It estimates nothing, and is merely a concrete measure of bases earned.

There is another statistic, called "PRO" and advocated in *Total Baseball*, which mathematically combines on-base percentage with slugging average. This is also a fairly simple formula, but has no inherent meaning, and is just another contrived number.

There is a good argument that *caught stealing* should be subtracted from *stolen bases*. I hesitated with the need to do so. We don't subtract getting thrown out stretching a double to a triple, getting doubled up, or getting out on a fielder's choice. But getting caught stealing certainly can take the wind out of a team's sails, so I decided to go along with including only net steals. I don't include sacrifices or hit by pitch, since they don't seem to be earned bases, but I'm sure some opinions will vary. There is also an argument that strikeouts should be weighted lower than putting the ball in play, since contact can advance a runner or force an error. Well, a strikeout is still better than a double play, and we just can't complicate this thing so far that no one can figure it out. Most of these other factors involve other players, and they certainly involve some subjectivity. I just want to simply measure the ability of a guy to earn bases when he *bats*.

Notions such as the effect of different baseball parks on a hitter's performance, the effect of age on those who stayed in the game past their great years, the effect of injuries and of wars all raise reasonable issues. They all had an impact. I'll take a crack at adjusting for the park effect, since it so clearly has a major impact. But age, injuries and wars are elements which have no place in formal statistics.

THE PARK EFFECT

What I'm about to do runs against my grain a bit. I don't mind at all moving away from the time-honored batting or slugging average to the more comprehensive earned bases average to measure hitting ability, but to start fooling around with something called "park effect" seemed silly at first. But once I found out how tremendous an effect the various stadiums had on offensive performance, I saw no choice. Park effect simply has to be put into the mix!

During the years Ted Williams played for Boston up in Fenway Park (excluding war years), the Red Sox and their opponents scored 17,537 runs. However, when the same teams played the same number of "away" games in the opponents' parks, only 15,440 runs were scored. This means that Fenway Park allowed 14.2 percent more offense than the other parks in the league. It makes sense when you consider "the green monster"—the huge green wall only 315 feet out into left field—and the fact that Fenway has relatively little foul territory.

Yankee Stadium, on the other hand, is clearly a pitcher's park. During the seventeen years Lou Gehrig played, there were 13,118 runs scored at Yankee Stadium, while the Yankees and their opponents scored 14,693 runs, a 10.7 percent increase, in opponents' parks. The distance from home plate to the backstop in Yankee Stadium is eighty-two feet, while in Fenway, which has the least foul territory in the majors, it is only sixty feet.

How do we deal with this? Well, is it fair to say Ted Williams was a better hitter than Gehrig just because he got the benefit of Fenway Park for half of his games, and Gehrig was stuck with Yankee Stadium? Williams hit for thirty-three points higher in his batting average at home, while Gehrig hit for twenty-two points lower when at Yankee Stadium. However, when we remove the home park effect, *Williams hit for a .328 average on the road while Gehrig hit .351*. Sure, the times were different, and Gehrig also got to play one-seventh of his road games at Fenway, but he clearly outhit Williams in neutral parks. However, Williams's earned bases average was .709 and Gehrig's was third on the all-time list at .701. (Ruth was out in a class by himself at .751.) What would Gehrig, also a lefty, have done if he had played at Fenway?

Let's take a look at some park differences. The two extremes today are the great hitter's park at Fenway Park in Boston and the pitcher's park at Oakland's Alameda County Coliseum. The park effect will be discussed more on page 18; it is basically number of runs scored in a park as compared to the average (100 percent).

Fenway Park, Boston

Yankee Stadium, New York

	FENWAY PARK	OAKLAND COLISEUM
PARK EFFECT	114%	88%
LEFT FIELD LINE	315	330
LEFT CENTER	379	372
DEEP CENTER	420	400
RIGHT CENTER	383	372
RIGHT FIELD LINE	302	330
BACKSTOP	60	90
FOUL TERRITORY	SMALLEST IN MAJORS	LARGEST IN MAJORS

The main difference in these figures seems to be foul territory, particularly the area behind home plate to the backstop. Fenway is actually bigger up the middle of the outfield, but is much smaller down both lines.

By the way, I'm sure the park effect varies somewhat for righties and lefties, although this matter has not yet been subjected to rigorous study, so detailed data is not yet available. The lesser foul territory behind the plate at Fenway helped both righties and lefties. There was an interesting theory advanced by Bill James that the "green monster" left field wall at Fenway also helped lefties, since pitchers would give them more pitches to pull to right (but pretty much stayed on the outside corner, away from righties).

My proposal is that we figure out how much of a player's EBA was affected by the park factor, and then add or subtract it from his average. I know this gets complicated, but it's too important to overlook. We know for instance that Fenway improved offensive production by 14.2 percent during the years Williams played. Parks are changed over time, fences are moved in and out, etc., so we need to measure it over a player's entire career.

We also need to keep in mind that the park effect only affected home games. Since Ted Williams played half of his games at Fenway, we can use only one-half of that 14.2 percent, or 7.1 percent to get to the net effect on his overall average. This means that if Ted played none of his games at Fenway, his average would have been 7.1 percent lower. However, all of Ted's opponents got to play at Fenway for at least one-seventh of their road games, and we can't deny Ted equal treatment. Therefore, we'll take away only six-sevenths of the net Fenway effect, leaving a final Fenway Park effect of 6.1 percent. We then multiply his .709 EBA times 6.1 percent to see how many of these percentage points were caused by Fenway's park effect. The result is a whopping forty-three points! So, Williams's EBA is reduced by forty-three points and his adjusted EBA is .666. The same type of calculation launches Gehrig into second place on the all-time list with an adjusted EBA of .733. The park factor I used also adjusts for the slight differences in half-innings played at home or away. Note that after the leagues expanded in 1961-62, and again in 1969 and 1977, players got fewer opportunities to play in other parks. However, I adjusted the park effects to reflect this factor.

THE EFFECT OF DIFFERENT TIMES

How do we compare a Babe Ruth, who played from 1914 to 1935, to a Willie Mays, who played from 1951 to 1973? They faced a different generation of pitchers and different rules about things such as loading up the balls with foreign substances, the old "spitball." Babe never had to hit a ball at night, a much tougher thing to do. And what about Ty Cobb? He played most of his 1905 to 1928 career during the era of the "dead ball," when baseballs were made of string wrapped around cork. What about the enlarged strike zone of the sixties, when the batting average dropped to about .245, nearly forty points lower than the .285 American League average of the twenties? The strike zone was first used in the 1860s to get pitchers to stop delaying games, but a pitch was considered outside the strike zone if it was over the head of the batter or if the ball struck the ground before reaching home plate. By 1907 the strike zone was "between the shoulders and the knees," and by 1950 it was "armpit to top of knee in the batter's natural stance." In 1963 it was enlarged to "top of the shoulder" (to Koufax's delight) until 1969 when it was lowered again to the armpit. In recent years, umps seem to have lowered it further, to just above the waist.

When the pitcher's mound was pushed back from 50 feet to 60.5 feet in 1893, the National League batting average, only .245 in 1892, rose to an all-time high of .309 in 1894. Fielding percentages in the early days, when fields were rutted and often unmowed and when balls were torn and scuffed, were below .900. Now they are routinely over .970.

Ty Cobb wrote poignantly in his autobiography *My Life in Baseball: The True Record* about some of the differences faced by old-timers. He wrote:

> *Split a finger in those days and you stuck it in the dirt and kept going. . . . In 1907, old Bennet Park in Detroit, as well as other arenas, sprouted grass which . . . was cow pasture rough and rutted with holes and soft spots. Where the infield grass met the skinned infield area, there were drop-offs that sent the ball flying in all directions. Diamonds were given a once over maybe once a week with a rake, . . . Drainage was crude and on wet days the outfield was marshy, if not worse. . . .*
>
> *In the old-time clubhouses we had nothing. Whirlpool baths, electrotherapy, skilled trainers . . . were luxuries the Wagners, LaJoies, Speakers, Mathewsons . . . never experienced. We put our uniforms on in primitive quarters, waited in line for the single shower to be vacated and dressed the next day in damp uniforms. That's right-damp, if not wet. Uniforms were jammed into containers after a game in their natural sweat soaked state and seldom saw a laundry. We wore them until they were a grimy disgrace.*
>
> *. . . We had no batting cages, motion pictures to record our form, pitching machines, coaching specialists, and multi-vitamin tablets. The pancake gloves we wore, the washboard fields we played on, the cramped upper berths we climbed into on endless rides over poor roadbeds, the need to wrestle with your own luggage, the four-men-to-one bathtub system in hotels, and the crude equipment. . . . For instance, bases were left out there until they were spiked apart. They weren't anchored or strapped down firmly and would shift a foot or more when you slid. Pitchers dosed the ball with licorice, talcum, slippery elm, and saliva flavored with tobacco. . . . If you tore a muscle or broke a bone, a long layoff was out of the question. You played whether you were sick, lame, or half blind from pain.*
>
> *The men I jousted with in the early years were a strange breed*

that will never be seen again. To them baseball was a way of life, their reason for existence. . . .

Ty wrote that back in 1961, and I surely don't know what he would have to say about today's megamillionaires. In any event, while I think we tend to exaggerate a bit the differences between the past and the present, we need to find a way to account for the clear differences when comparing players from various eras. We often hear that today's players are better than yesterday's, but old-timers often say the opposite. Hall of Famer Joe Sewell told *Legends of Baseball*, "You know if Ty Cobb were playing today on those artificial surfaces the way he played in his prime, he'd hit closer to .500 than to .400."

We know a player is great because he stands out from other players of his time. *Therefore, I submit that the greatest hitters of all time should be the ones who stood out farthest in front of the players of their own day.* Babe Ruth had a lifetime EBA of .764 (adjusted upward thirteen points for the park effect). The average player from 1914 to 1935 had an EBA of .443. Thus, the Babe had an earned bases average an astounding 172 percent higher than the average player of his time. He is far and away the greatest hitter of all time. Lou Gehrig comes in at second place with an adjusted EBA of .723, which is 261 points higher than the .462 average of his own era (1923 to 1939). The table on page 22 plots the average EBA for each ten-year period since 1871.

THE SUPER ULTIMATE STATISTIC

I propose that the greatest hitters of all time be measured by the extent to which their earned bases average, adjusted for park effects, exceeds the league average during the years they played. The sabermetricians call this *normalizing* to the league average. This statistic should create a strong presumption about a player's offensive rank, but not an irrefutable presumption. As we said earlier, no statistic can pick up the intangibles, so the final ranking still is open to some debate.

SABERMETRIC STATISTICS

Earlier I reviewed the statistical measurements proposed by members of SABR. The work of this group and its statistical

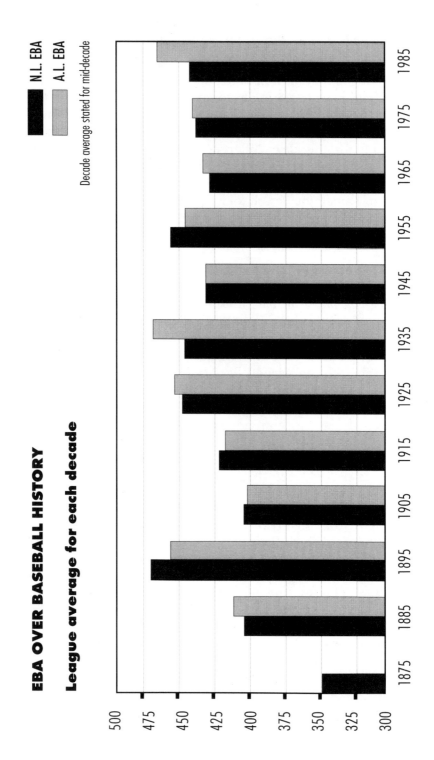

EBA OVER BASEBALL HISTORY

League average for each decade

N.L. EBA
A.L. EBA

Decade average stated for mid-decade

progeny has revolutionized analysis of the game. But, as I said, I believe the weighted and complicated formula estimates they present are difficult for most fans. Moreover, the "estimated" values they present are not tangible or real, and they devalue the extra bases earned by the sluggers and by the speedsters in favor of an emphasis on the singles slappers. Surely the fans out in Kiner's Korner in Pittsburgh did not hang around in a lost game for Kiner's last at bat just to see some singles! I don't mean to be critical, and I refer to these statistics in close cases, but they are too complicated and many times are just clearly wrong.

Probably the most favored statistic of sabermetrics for measuring a hitter's performance is the *linear weights measure of batting runs*, which measures the estimated number of runs generated by a batter over and above what the average batter would have gotten. The central premise is that baseball is all about generating runs and so batters should be measured by the number of runs they generate. They have developed a statistic which "weights" the possible run-producing events, such as singles, doubles, walks, steals, etc.; that is, they measure the average number of runs generated by each of them. They subtract outs. They claim that the weights derived in their formula will correctly match, within a few percentage points, the actual number of runs a team scores. Therefore, they argue that applying this statistic to an individual batter, even though we can never determine how many runs he *actually* generated, yields what is likely a good estimate of the number of runs he was responsible for.

The statistic is as follows. The "weights" are shown in the parentheses:

$$\text{Runs generated} = (.47)1B + (.78)2B + (1.09)3B + (1.40)HR + (.33)(BB + HB) - (.25)(AB\text{-}H) - (.50)OOB$$

This statistic is similar to the EBA in some respects. However, it *weights* the various batting events, and does not include net steals (sorry Rickey!). It also subtracts outs at bat (AB-H), and outs on base (OOB). A problem with it is that it cannot cover all of baseball's history. It is obvious that the walks and particularly the steals and baserunning of the early days were more important than today. So, the weights, if we assume we need weights (I don't), should be different for the early days. The other problem with this statistic is that it favors long careers, since the "batting runs" statistic is cumulative. This is why Ty Cobb's total is so high.

The All-Time Dream Team requires a statistic for all time, and the sabermetric formula relates only to the past sixty or so years. Perhaps it is more precise for the modern era, but it has no place before 1920. Thus it is useless for the purposes of this book. I do include this statistic in my tables as ADJ./ BR, which is the estimated number of batted runs generated beyond that estimated for the average player during a given career, and it too is adjusted for the park effect. I'll also examine its meaning as we determine our dream team lineup. It can't hurt to look at everything.

THE BEST HITTERS

The table on page 26 will rank in order of relative adjusted earned bases average the fifty best hitters who ever lived. Underlined figures represent that the data is unavailable for some part of the player's career. Any individual statistics in the top three ever are listed in bold. Guess who comes out *numero uno?*

FINAL OFFENSIVE RANKING: THE STAR SYSTEM

In the chapters on each individual position, I will present the final candidates for that position, ranked according to hitting, defense and opinion poll results. As I said earlier, the EBA ranking carries with it a strong presumption as to the player's rank as a hitter, one which should not be easily overcome. However, we must agree that the EBA does not capture everything. We cannot completely remove the human element from the process, and so we get one last shot at accepting or modifying the ranking established by the EBA. It is of assistance to further categorize the players by what I call the "Star" rating. This approach will help me draw a line between the very best and the other greats who are close below. Basically, I divide players into categories such as the best ever, exceptional, above average, average, and below average. The utility of this system will become apparent as I evaluate individual positions later on, particularly since some great hitters are only average fielders. This approach also has the benefit of providing a rational method for deviating from the EBA ranking where needed.

For batting, the system is as follows:

4 Stars designate the few players who defined the offensive standard for all others, those who transcended the game, and whose accomplishments will last in memory for all time. This rating is reserved for those whose adjusted EBA is 145 percent or better than the average player of the time. Only Babe Ruth (best of all time), Lou Gehrig (put the "power" in power hitting), Mickey Mantle (consistently hit awesome homers, many out of the park), Ted Williams (best pure hitter ever, two triple crowns), Willie Mays (best all-around player), and Jimmie Foxx (534 HR, .325 BA) receive a 4-Star rating. I have no reason to change their ranks. I draw the line at DiMaggio since his 369 homers, thirty steals and .325 BA together do not quite compare with the top guys, and so it's a natural point of separation. As confirmation, the sabermetric guys only give Joe a 507, half of what the leaders scored.

However, there are definitely a few names missing here. In recognition of his career .367 batting average, his 891 stolen bases, his 1,249/357 strikeout-to-walk ratio, and his consistency for more than two decades, I include Ty Cobb in the 4-Star rating. His sabermetric rating is over 1,000. I won't jack him up over the other 4-Star guys, but he gets seventh place. I'm also bringing up Rogers Hornsby (.358 BA, two triple crowns, .577 SA). I considered the great Hank Aaron, whose 755 home runs demand a second look. However, Hank's home-run percentage was only thirteenth of all time, and his .305 BA and other stats (167 net steals) don't really justify a fourth star. Similiar is the case of Pete Rose, who was an exceptional, but certainly not a 4-Star, hitter. Pete just hung around long enough to get the record for most hits ever. Endurance records are great, but we need more for four stars. Only a percent or two separate Cobb and Hornsby from those above them on the EBA rating, and they clearly belong in the 4-Star club.

3 Stars for exceptional hitting ability are awarded to all players whose EBA is 125 percent or better than the average EBA during their career. Forty-five players fall into this cate-

THE TOP FIFTY BEST HITTERS OF ALL TIME

PLAYER	YEARS	POS	TEAM	AB	H	2B	3B	HR	RBI	BB
1. Babe RUTH	1914-35	RF	NY	8,399	2,873	506	136	**714**	**2,211**	**2,056**
2. Lou GEHRIG	1923-39	1B	NY	8,001	2,721	534	163	493	1,990	1,508
3. Mickey MANTLE	1951-68	CF	NY	8,102	2,415	344	72	536	1,509	1,734
4. Ted WILLIAMS	1939-60	LF	BOS	7,706	2,654	525	71	521	1,839	**2,019**
5. Willie MAYS	1951-73	CF	GIANTS	10,881	3,283	523	140	**660**	1,903	1,463
6. Jimmie FOXX	1925-45	1B	PHI/BOS	8,134	2,646	458	125	534	1,921	1,452
7. Joe DIMAGGIO	1936-51	CF	NY	6,821	2,214	389	131	361	1,537	790
8. Rickey HENDERSON	1979-(93)	LF	OAK/NY/TOR	7,356	2,137	351	56	221	784	1,405
9. Ty COBB	1905-28	CF	DET	11,434	**4,190**	724	**295**	117	1,937	1,249
10. Frank ROBINSON	1956-76	LF	CIN/BAL	10,006	2,943	528	72	586	1,812	1,420
11. Dick ALLEN	1963-77	1B	PHI	6,332	1,848	320	79	351	1,119	894
12. Rogers HORNSBY	1915-37	2B	STL	8,173	2,930	541	169	301	1,584	1,038
13. Hank AARON	1954-76	RF	BVS/MIL	**12,364**	**3,371**	624	98	**755**	**2,297**	1,407
14. Johnny MIZE	1936-53	1B	STL/NY	6,443	2,011	367	83	359	1,337	856
15. Mel OTT	1926-47	RF	GIANTS	9,456	2,876	488	72	511	1,860	1,708
16. Joe JACKSON	1908-20	LF	CLE/CHI	4,981	1,774	307	168	54	785	519
17. Hank GREENBERG	1930-47	1B	DET	5,193	1,628	379	71	331	1,276	882
18. Darryl STRAWBERRY	1983-(93)	RF	METS/LA	4,664	1,210	219	34	290	969	690
19. Eddie MATHEWS	1952-68	3B	MIL	8,537	2,315	354	72	512	1,453	1,444
20. Willie McCOVEY	1959-80	1B	SF	8,197	2,211	353	46	521	1,555	1,345
21. Dan BROUTHERS	1879-04	1B	BUF	6,716	2,304	461	206	106	1,056	840
22. Stan MUSIAL	1941-63	1B	STL	10,972	3,630	**725**	177	475	1,951	1,599
23. Honus WAGNER	1897-17	SS	PIT	10,430	3,415	640	**252**	101	1,732	963
24. Tris SPEAKER	1907-28	CF	BOS/CLE	10,208	3,514	792	222	117	1,529	1,381
25. Joe MORGAN	1963-84	2B	CIN	9,277	2,517	449	96	268	1,133	**1,865**

SO	SB/CS	BA	SA	ADJ. BR	EBA	LEAGUE EBA	PARK EFF.	MVP	TRIP. CRWN.	RK. YR.	ADJ. EBA	% AHEAD OF HIS TIMES
1,330	123/118	.342	.690	1,355	.751	.443	95.1%	1			.764	172%
789	102/101	.340	.632	966	.691	.462	89.2%	2	1		.723	156%
1,710	153/38	.298	.557	838	.647	.438	90.6%	3	1		.672	153%
709	24/17	.344	.634	1,093	.709	.447	114.2%	2	2		.666	149%
1,526	338/103	.302	.557	838	.629	.438	96.4%	2		*	.639	146%
1,311	88/72	.325	.609	768	.670	.457	101.9%	3	1		.665	146%
369	30/9	.325	.579	507	.625	.457	89.0%	3			.654	143%
1,052	1,095/248	.291	.444	458	.629	.460	89.8%	1			.658	143%
357	891/178	.367	.513	1,018	.616	.426	103.7%	1	1		.606	142%
1,532	204/77	.294	.537	754	.606	.435	95.8%	2	1	*	.618	142%
1,556	133/52	.292	.534	469	.603	.431	97.0%	1		*	.611	142%
679	135/64	.358	.577	859	.632	.443	101.6%	2	2		.627	142%
1,383	240/73	.305	.555	903	.612	.437	98.1%	1			.617	141%
524	28/1	.312	.562	505	.617	.441	99.0%				.620	141%
896	89/NA	.304	.533	773	.613	.442	97.0%	1			.621	140%
158	202/61	.356	.518	440	.589	.415	102.8%				.582	140%
844	58/26	.313	.605	440	.666	.459	109.1%	2			.640	139%
1,138	205/84	.259	.508	258	.594	.449	92.4%			*	.615	137%
1,487	68/39	.271	.509	531	.583	.445	89.8%				.609	137%
1,550	26/22	.270	.515	538	.584	.435	96.0%	1			.594	137%
238	235/NA	.343	.520	632	.607	.443	102.3%				.601	136%
696	78/31	.331	.559	930	.619	.445	106.1%	3			.603	136%
327	722/15	.327	.466	652	.573	.424	99.3%				.574	135%
220	433/129	.345	.500	813	.586	.429	103.0%	1			.578	135%
1,015	689/162	.271	.427	470	.570	.434	90.6%	2			.584	135%

THE TOP FIFTY BEST HITTERS OF ALL TIME

PLAYER	YEARS	POS	TEAM	AB	H	2B	3B	HR	RBI	BB
26. Harry STOVEY	1880-93	CF	PHI/BOS	6,138	1,769	347	174	122	<u>549</u>	661
27. Duke SNIDER	1947-64	CF	BKN/LA	7,161	2,116	358	85	407	1,333	971
28. Mike SCHMIDT	1972-89	3B	PHI	8,352	2,234	408	59	548	1,595	1,507
29. Willie STARGELL	1962-82	1B	PIT	7,927	2,232	423	55	475	1,540	937
30. Ross BARNES	1871-78	2B	BOS/CHI	1,032	329	45	17	2	111	59
31. Dolph CAMILLI	1933-45	1B	PHI/BRO	5,353	1,482	261	86	239	950	947
32. Ralph KINER	1946-55	LF	PIT	5,205	1,451	216	34	369	1,015	1,011
33. Harmon KILLEBREW	1954-75	1B	WAS/MIN	8,147	2,086	290	24	573	1,584	1,559
34. Wally BERGER	1930-40	OF	BOS	5,163	1,550	255	59	242	898	435
35. Babe HERMAN	1926-45	CF	BRO	5,603	1,818	399	110	181	997	520
36. Hack WILSON	1923-34	CF	CHI	4,760	1,461	266	67	244	1,062	674
37. Reggie JACKSON	1967-87	RF	OAK/NY	9,864	2,584	463	49	563	1,702	1,375
38. Ken WILLIAMS	1915-29	RF	STL	5,481	1,552	242	138	49	796	474
39. Pete BROWNING	1882-94	CF	LOU	4,820	1,646	295	85	46	<u>353</u>	466
40. Roger CONNOR	1880-97	1B	NY	7,794	2,467	441	233	138	1,322	1,002
41. Billy HAMILTON	1888-01	LF	PHI/BOS	6,284	2,163	242	94	40	736	1,187
42. Harry HEILMANN	1914-32	RF	DET	7,787	2,660	542	151	183	1,539	856
43. Eddie COLLINS	1906-30	2B	PHI/CHI	9,949	3,311	437	187	47	1,299	1,499
44. Frank HOWARD	1958-73	RF	LA/WAS	6,488	1,774	245	35	382	1,119	782
45. Al SIMMONS	1924-44	OF	PHI	8,759	2,927	539	149	307	1,827	615
46. Chuck KLEIN	1928-44	OF	PHI	6,486	2,076	398	74	300	1,201	601
47. Nap LAJOIE	1896-16	2B	PHI/CLE	9,589	3,242	657	163	83	1,599	516
48. Ed DELAHANTY	1888-03	OF	PHI	7,505	2,597	522	185	101	1,464	741
49. Norm CASH	1958-74	1B	DET	6,705	1,820	241	41	377	1,043	1,091
50. Hal TROSKY	1933-46	1B	CLE	5,161	1,561	331	58	228	1,012	545

SO	SB/CS	BA	SA	ADJ. BR	EBA	LEAGUE EBA	PARK EFF.	MVP	TRIP. CRWN.	RK. YR.	ADJ. EBA	% AHEAD OF HIS TIMES
323	509/NA	.288	.461	320	.588	.426	106.1%				.573	135%
1,237	99/50	.295	.540	405	.601	.451	98.1%				.606	134%
1,883	174/92	.267	.527	561	.608	.440	106.1%	3			.591	134%
1,936	17/16	.282	.529	485	.580	.433	101.4%	1			.577	133%
53	11/NA	.319	.407	48	.496	.353	113.7%				.468	133%
961	60/NA	.277	.492	277	.578	.429	104.0%	1			.568	132%
749	22/2	.279	.548	373	.625	.452	110.0%				.598	132%
1,699	19/18	.256	.509	500	.589	.436	103.4%	1			.575	132%
694	36/NA	.300	.522	255	.565	.444	92.3%				.584	132%
553	94/NA	.324	.532	318	.587	.453	103.0%				.595	131%
713	52/5	.307	.545	310	.610	.453	106.5%				.593	131%
2,597	228/115	.262	.490	503	.562	.447	91.1%	1			.583	130%
287	154/105	.319	.530	253	.588	.441	105.8%				.573	130%
167	258/NA	.341	.467	388	.562	.444	95.3%				.573	129%
449	244/NA	.317	.486	564	.572	.448	98.6%				.576	128%
218	937/NA	.344	.432	448	.645	.465	117.3%				.597	128%
550	112/64	.342	.520	527	.574	.444	101.6%				.570	128%
286	744/173	.333	.428	604	.553	.431	100.0%	1			.553	128%
1,460	8/9	.273	.499	344	.552	.432	99.6%				.552	128%
737	87/67	.334	.535	399	.567	.443	100.1%				.566	128%
521	79/NA	.320	.543	330	.582	.442	105.0%	1	1		.565	128%
85	380/21	.338	.467	567	.529	.425	96.0%		1		.538	127%
244	455/NA	.346	.505	550	.605	.461	107.9%				.584	127%
1,091	43/30	.271	.488	390	.559	.433	104.1%				.549	127%
440	28/23	.302	.522	208	.568	.459	95.6%				.579	126%

gory. I'm making one adjustment here, bringing in Stan Musial. He had nearly double the at bats of the other first basemen in the 3-Star category, over his tremendous twenty-two year career. He also is the all-time leader in doubles and received three MVP awards. This certainly puts him ahead of Allen, Mize and Greenberg. It's not quite enough, however, for a fourth star. He is not in Gehrig's class, and even Foxx got fifty more homers in nearly 3,000 fewer at bats.

2 Stars designate above-average hitting. Players with an EBA more than 110 percent of the average of the times get this rating.

1 Star goes to any player with an EBA higher than the average range of his time.

BEST HITTERS AT EACH POSITION

The bottom line! Don't forget, this is just hitting. For the final dream team we need to consider other qualities like defense and intangibles. Here are the players, first and second place, with their Star rating.

Babe Ruth trots home after hitting a home run.

FIRST BASE	Lou Gehrig ****
	Jimmie Foxx ****
SECOND BASE	Rogers Hornsby ****
	Joe Morgan ***
THIRD BASE	Eddie Mathews ***
	Mike Schmidt ***
SHORTSTOP	Honus Wagner ***
	Arky Vaughan **
CATCHER	Buck Ewing ***
	Bill Dickey **
OUTFIELD	Babe Ruth ****
	Ted Williams ****
	Mickey Mantle ****
	Willie Mays ****
	Ty Cobb ****
	Joe DiMaggio ***

Chapter Three

Fielding

I f baseball rules allowed a platoon system for offense and defense, most of the great hitters in the previous chapter, with the clear exception of Willie Mays, would be sitting out half the game on the All-Time Dream Team.

Instead, we might see a Keith Hernandez at first base, Bill Mazeroski at second, and Bill Dahlen or Ozzie Smith at shortstop. Brooks Robinson would likely take third, and Richie Ashburn and Max Carey would find time in the outfield.

Who are the best defensive players ever? The answer to that question will never be found in a simple number, and may just be lost to the ages. As I said earlier, baseball is about hitting! That's what we love about it. Sure, there is beauty in a precise double play or a diving catch in the outfield. I loved to see Roberto Clemente, Jesse Barfield or Dave Winfield gun down a runner at the plate from right field. But the fascination has always been with what goes on in the batter's box. So, the statisticians and awards-givers focus on hitting—and have for most of baseball's existence. The weakness of defensive stats is itself an indication of the preeminence of hitting.

We do have a few numbers to work with. The time-honored fielding percentage measures the percentage of errorless plays, by dividing successful plays (putouts and assists) by the number of chances. I believe the number of putouts and assists *per game* are generally the most powerful yardsticks of defensive ability. Putouts tell us something about how often a player *got to* the ball, a measure of speed and timing, and assists tell us that plus a lot about the power and accuracy of a player's arm. The sabermetricians have developed a rather complicated, but not too useful, stat that combines various fielding stats and "normalizes," that is, compares them against the league average. Thorn and Palmer include this statistic in *Total Baseball*. Called *fielding runs*, this statistic purports to measure the runs saved by a player's defensive play. My concern is that it misses by a mile in some instances. For example, Hal Chase was widely regarded as the best defensive first baseman in the first fifty years of baseball (when he wasn't intentionally dropping the ball), but Chase came up with a negative score with the sabermetric formula. Brooks Robinson, probably the best defensive third baseman ever, is not even in the top ten in fielding runs saved. It does seem to work loosely, however, so I consider it cautiously.

We also have the Gold Glove awards, which started in 1957. These awards are the first attempt to annually identify the best defensive player at each position. But they have been criticized for often looking only at players who also compiled decent offensive numbers. *Que sera sera!*

What we really need is a stat which records the opposite of errors, that is, the great plays, the plays which the average player would not have made. J. Roy Stockton wrote of such a play when the great first baseman George Sisler, with a man on third, anticipated a squeeze bunt and, with magnificent timing and speed, charged toward home. He fielded the bunt, tagged the batter on the run, and flipped to the catcher for the play at home. The great overhead catch by Willie Mays of Vic Wertz's shot to deep center in the 1954 World Series is often depicted as one of the all-time great defensive plays. And many of us remember Brooks Robinson's incredible dives along the third-base line to snare would-be doubles.

But until such a measurement comes along, we must use what data we have and look back to the views of those knowledgeable about the game — those who saw the players and recorded their observations.

This book is not an effort to present the greatest *defensive* players ever. My interest is in the greatest *players* ever. The fact that I require Hall of Famers will eliminate some outstanding defensive players who could not hit. Marty Marion,

"Mr. Shortstop," is one example. I've included the stats of players like Marion to prove my point, but upon further analysis they quickly pale in the face of the great fielders who could also hit.

A great hitter who is not also a great fielder can make the dream team. This is particularly true for outfielders and first basemen, as we will see with Babe Ruth, Ty Cobb or Lou Gehrig. However, the converse will generally not be the case, even at the primarily defensive positions of second base or shortstop. Bill Mazerowski is a case in point. He was one of the best, if not the best, defensive second basemen ever. He is "second" on Thorn and Palmer's "defensive games won" lists for all positions, using sabermetric formulas. He was, however, an average hitter, batting .260 lifetime. He was certainly no slugger, and had an EBA of only .402. Therefore, surveys of the great second basemen do not list Mazerowski among the top several second sackers of all time. He is not in the Hall of Fame, and has received only about 40 percent of the votes needed in each of the last several years. I hope he makes it in, but it is certainly a stark indication of the preeminence of hitting that the best fielding second baseman ever is not in the Hall of Fame. Keith Hernandez is often called the best defensive first baseman ever, and is first on the sabermetric defensive formula for that position. But, while a very good hitter, he also is not on my Top Fifty Hitters list. No one would argue for him on the All-Time Dream Team over the likes of Gehrig, Foxx and Sisler.

The following tables present fielding stats for each position. The statistics presented are only for the position primarily played during a player's career, and only for games played at that position. Keep in mind that fielding stats vary according to position. Third base is the most difficult defensive position and so it has the lowest fielding percentages. Stats generally improve as one moves around the horn to the right. I have sorted the players by position for ease of analysis, but they are ranked according to batting prowess.

For the fielding positions, second base, shortstop and third base, I have also included the stats for those Hall of Famers who were not on my Top Fifty Hitters list, but who have been identified in some surveys as one of the best ever at a given position. In the individual chapters on each position I'll discuss how we got to the "short list" of candidates for each position.

A couple of comments about the defensive tables. I included a few different statistics for each position. As I've stated several times, the numbers just don't do the job on defense, but there are ways we can maximize what they say. The fielding runs formula is given, and I've already discussed its marginal utility. Gold Gloves are also listed where applicable (after 1954). The utility of fielding percentage, putouts (PO), assists (A), errors (E) and double plays (DP) vary for each position. Where they are of significant help, I will also include the stats *per game*, e.g., PO/G means putouts per game, A/G means assists per game.

Outfielders are best measured by fielding percentage and by putouts per game. The fielding percentage will weed out the bad gloves, and a high putout-per-game ratio will tell us something about how many balls they were able to catch up to. The better fielders like Mays and DiMaggio naturally got under many balls that others would not have reached, and this clearly shows in their putouts per game. Assists will tell us a bit about arm strength for outfielders, but the number of assists is so low compared to the number of games that it seems of less real impact and should receive less weight. Of course, we need to adjust for the bad field conditions of the early days, so we need to compare the various stats against the average performance of the times.

First basemen have the most useless statistics, since the *putouts* statistic is dominated by the catches they make of balls thrown (theoretically) right at them. I guess all we really have of significant utility is the fielding percentage and, perhaps, assists.

Second base, shortstop and third base get more mileage out of the defensive stats, since the putouts and assists per game are good measures of how many balls these players got to, and what kind of power and accuracy was in their arms. Double plays per game are very important since we want these guys to clear the bases for us whenever possible.

Catchers are generally regarded for their ability to control the pitcher, keep him on an even keel. Of course, there is no objective way to measure this quality. Passed ball statistics are not generally available, so the best measure we have is assists, which tell us more about the catcher's arm. Therefore, I will use assists per game to pick up how many runners, either stealing or bunting, catchers threw out. Unfortunately, strike-outs are recorded as putouts for catchers, so we dilute beyond any recognition the only measure of their ability to catch foul pops and make plays at the plate.

The following sections will present defensive stats for each position and will compare some of the stats to league averages during a player's career, so we can see how far ahead they stood from the average player of the time.

In order to help distinguish fielders, I have again used a **Star** rating. As discussed for batting, the star system basically helps to draw lines between great fielders and those who were only above average, or average. While it's important to rank players, as we do, the star system helps to put these rankings in perspective. A **4-Star** player is one of the best of all time at the position, a player who defined the standard for the position, at least for his era. While a few players could qualify for the rating, it is only given to those who were great in every aspect of the position: speed, arm, glove, savvy. A **3-Star** player is exceptional in most categories and weak in none, a truly great and distinguished fielder. A **2-Star** fielder is significantly above average. A **1-Star** player is in the average range, and **0-Star** designates below-average fielding overall.

To analyze this data more closely, I needed to compare each player directly against players of his own era—that is, his contemporaries during his career. I included in this process only players who were primarily outfielders, who played at least five years at the position, and whose careers were wholly within the time period of the player being compared. In effect, I compared each candidate with the journeymen outfielders of their day!

The patterns were interesting. Fielding percentages rose, as fields and gloves improved, from about .958 on average during Cobb's time to about .979 during Rickey Henderson's. Putouts per game rose as the game moved more to the out-field, from 1.95 during Cobb's time to about 2.24 during Ott's career. They've dipped a bit since 1950, probably as outfield

OUTFIELD DEFENSIVE RANKINGS

Players listed chronologically. Numbers next to names relate to my Top Fifty Hitters ranking.

PLAYER	GAMES	FA	PO/G	A	E	DP	FR	GOLD GLOVES
26. STOVEY	944	.896	1,801/1.9	165	229	33	42	NA
39. BROWNING	998	.883	1,892/1.9	143	269	36	-5	NA
41. HAMILTON	1,584	.926	3,444/2.2	182	288	55	-7	NA
9. COBB	2,935	961	6,361/2.2	392	271	107	54	NA
24. SPEAKER	2,698	.970	6,787/2.5	448	222	139	245	NA
16. J. JACKSON	1,289	.962	2,362/1.8	183	100	36	24	NA
42. HEILMANN	1,594	.962	2,794/1.8	183	117	42	-31	NA
15. OTT	2,313	.980	4,511/2.0	256	86	60	-27	NA
1. RUTH	2,241	.968	4,444/2.0	204	155	48	-4	NA
38. K. WILLIAMS	1,298	.958	2,948/2.3	167	137	40	52	NA
36. H. WILSON	1,257	.965	2,810/2.2	98	105	28	-76	NA
35. HERMAN	1,185	.961	2,270/1.9	106	101	21	-46	NA
46. KLEIN	1,600	.962	3,250/2.0	194	135	39	7	NA
34. BERGER	1,296	.974	3,324/2.6	87	102	21	-6	NA
7. DIMAGGIO	1,721	.978	4,516/2.6	153	105	30	16	NA
4. WILLIAMS	2,151	.974	4,158/1.9	140	113	30	-67	NA
32. KINER	1,382	.974	2,875/2.1	80	88	14	-30	NA
27. SNIDER	1,918	.985	4,099/2.1	123	66	18	-79	NA
3. MANTLE	2,019	.982	4,438/2.2	117	82	27	-99	1
5. MAYS	2,843	.981	7,095/2.5	195	141	60	91	12
13. AARON	2,760	.980	5,539/2.0	201	117	41	65	3
NL CLEMENTE	2,370	.973	4,696/2.0	266	140	42	160	12
10. F. ROBINSON	2,132	.984	3,978/1.9	135	68	26	37	0
44. HOWARD	1,435	.975	2,114/1.5	82	58	12	-87	0
37. R. JACKSON	2,102	.967	4,062/1.9	133	142	31	-30	0
8. HENDERSON	1,880	.979	4,754/2.5	102	102	17	103	1
18. STRAWBERRY	1,288	.977	2,360/1.8	72	56	22	23	0

fences started moving in. I believe putouts per game is the best measure for outfielders, since it measures how many balls per game they were able to get to, relative to other outfielders. Assists per game, a measure of an outfielder's arm, were higher back in Cobb's time (.14 per game), when the outfielders could play closer to the base paths, but, with the advent of the lively ball, they dropped steadily over time to the current level of .07 per game.

I then compared how far beyond the average of their time each player's personal stats were. The data on page 40 subtract the league's fielding percentage from the player's. Columns three and four divide the players' putouts and assists per game by the league average during their careers. I've shortened the list of candidates to those outfielders who are among my top twenty-five batters, and a few more who are suggested by various opinion polls (see chapter five for details).

I like this approach better than the sabermetric equation, since we can view each stat separately. I don't include double plays (which are big in the fielding runs stat for some reason), since we *are* dealing with the outfield.

4-Star Outfielders. Two outfielders on our short list clearly qualify. Willie Mays and Tris Speaker defined the position! They had no weaknesses and excelled in every category — sureness of glove, speed, savvy, and a powerful arm. Speaker was the overwhelming defensive winner in the first fifty years of baseball, even over DiMaggio. Mays is the modern day Gold Glove king, and a 1987 survey for the book *Players' Choice* voted him the clear all-time favorite defensively. Mays is the popular choice for all-time best glove, and the numbers back it up. It is clear that Mays and Speaker were in a class by themselves. I give Willie the edge over Tris, as do the numbers. Of course, there are other 4-Star fielders, even though they're not candidates for all-time honors. One is Richie Ashburn, who led the league nine times in putouts with an astounding 2.9 per game.

3-Star Outfielders. Joe DiMaggio is an obvious choice for third place on the short list, finishing strong in the *Players' Choice* survey and in most of the literature. Some will argue for a fourth star. He amazed fans with his grace and seeming

Tris Speaker

effortlessness as he anticipated outfield flys as well as anyone ever did. His putouts per game were super, but his arm was not quite good enough to compete with Willie and Tris, and his fielding percentage was just average, so three stars is all I

Percentage Comparison of Fielding Stats of Final Outfield Candidates Compared to the Average Player of the Time

PLAYER	HIS FIELDING AVG. MINUS LEAGUE AVER.	HIS PUTOUTS PER GAME DIVIDED BY LEAGUE	HIS ASSISTS PER GAME DIVIDED BY LEAGUE AVER.
MAYS	+.004	+38%	+18%
SPEAKER	+.012	+28%	+16%
DIMAGGIO	+.001	+22%	+ 8%
CLEMENTE	−.004	+ 9%	+94%
MANTLE	+.005	+21%	0%
AARON	+.003	+11%	+26%
HENDERSON	+.000	+28%	−18%
F. ROBINSON	+.007	+ 3%	+ 9%
OTT	+.006	−13%	+33%
COBB	−.003	+11%	− 7%
RUTH	+.001	−11%	− 4%
WILLIAMS	−.003	−10%	− 3%
STRAWBERRY	−.002	− 8%	−15%

can justify. Roberto Clemente's twelve Gold Gloves, matched only by Mays for outfielders (although the award was not given until Mays's seventh year), easily gains him a fourth place. He had only an average fielding percentage and only 2.0 putouts per game (just a little above average, probably the reason he was not a center fielder). I'm tempted to give his "golden arm" a fourth star, but my rule is that putouts are the primary measure in the outfield. Clemente's arm was an awesome thing to behold in action, the best ever, as testified to by those who knew him and as demonstrated by his astonishing 266 assists. His assists per game were nearly double that of his contemporaries. DiMaggio and Clemente define the next class of outfielder.

2-Star Outfielders. Mickey Mantle got under a lot of balls while his legs held up. He was a former shortstop and so combined a great glove with great speed. His arm was only average, and the speed left somewhat as the crippled knees sapped his greatness. Clearly, however, the Mick was well above average. In fact, his glove was surer than DiMaggio's, and his putouts as good. A slightly better arm would have easily given the Mick a third star. He had one Gold Glove to his credit. I rank Henry Aaron in sixth place and include him in this class, although also not a center fielder. Henry combined a well-above-average putout rate, a sound glove, and one of the best arms ever. Rickey Henderson also got to a lot of balls with his great speed—second only to Mays in this category. But he had a well-below-average arm, and an average glove. Overall, however, Rickey's speed, the prototype for a left fielder, and sure glove (notwithstanding that cockamamie swoop move he made to hotdog pop-ups) clearly make him well above average. He needed a better arm to get another star. Frank Robinson and Mel Ott were known mainly for what they did with their great bats, and had only average putouts. But both had great gloves and powerful arms, and just made it into the 2-Star class.

1-Star Outfielders. Ty Cobb is called "the most spectacular outfielder of his time" by Harry Grayson in his *They Played the Game*, noting how Cobb once threw out three runners at first base in one game from right field. It was a different game then, a closer game with the dead ball. However, here is a place where the myth has perhaps overtaken the facts, and I don't intend to be swept up by the myth. His defensive ability was often disputed by those who played with him, and he certainly did not have a great arm. Cobb himself admitted this. He explained it by noting that he had a good arm early in his career, but hurt it trying to become a pitcher, learning trick pitches. The statistics back up the latter view, as he had an average fielding percentage, an above-average rate of putouts, and a slightly below-average arm (assists). It's a close call. I give him tenth place and an overall average rating. Babe Ruth is under average, but not quite low enough to lose one star. His glove and arm were average and his putouts below average, but he hangs on to one star.

O-Star Outfielders. Ted Williams must be placed in the below-average class, since his putouts per game were well below average, and he had negative marks in fielding and assists.

FIRST BASE DEFENSIVE RANKINGS

Players listed in chronological order. Numbers next to names relate to my Top Fifty Hitters ranking. *NL* indicates the individual is not listed on the top-fifty list.

PLAYER	GAMES	FA	PO	A/G	E/G	DP	FR	GOLD GLOVES
21. BROUTHERS	1,633	.971	16,365	654/.57	512/.31	890	-15	NA
40. R. CONNOR	1,758	.978	17,605	856/.49	419/.24	955	48	NA
NL SISLER	1,971	.987	18,837	1,529/.78	269/.14	1,468	89	NA
NL TERRY	1,579	.992	15,972	1,108/.70	138/.09	1,334	67	NA
2. GEHRIG	2,137	.991	19,510	1,087/.51	193/.09	1,574	-59	NA
6. FOXX	1,919	.992	17,207	1,222/.64	155/.08	1,528	43	NA
17. GREENBERG	1,138	.991	10,564	724/.64	104/.09	973	24	NA
31. CAMILLI	1,476	.990	13,724	957/.65	141/.10	1,189	2	2
50. TROSKY	1,321	.991	12,124	752/.57	121/.09	1,146	-13	NA
14. MIZE	1,667	.992	14,850	1,032/.62	133/.08	1,320	-11	NA
22. MUSIAL	1,016	.992	8,709	688/.68	78/.08	935	3	NA
33. KILLEBREW	969	.992	7,521	555/.57	69/.09	678	-4	0
20. MCCOVEY	2,045	.987	17,170	1,222/.60	233/.11	1,405	-21	0
29. STARGELL	848	.991	7,293	384/.45	67/.08	701	-54	0
11. ALLEN	807	.989	6,747	418/.52	82/.10	640	-32	0
NL MURRAY	2,365	.993	20,837	1,826/.77	161/.07	1,998	58	3

He really only cared about hitting, anyway. Darryl Strawberry? Well, we all have seen him at work! Enough said.

FIRST BASE DEFENSE

Defense for first base is nearly impossible to evaluate from the numbers. Putouts are a reflection of balls thrown directly to the player to get a force-out at first. Unassisted putouts per game would be useful, but are not available. Fielding percentages are inflated likewise by the putouts. So, the best stats are probably assists per game and errors per game.

I checked the fielding stats of a random number of journeymen first basemen over the years. It was difficult to do since first base is such a vagabond position. Not many guys make a career out of it, and it is often used to hide an injured or

PLAYER	NUMBER OF TIMES LED LEAGUE					A/G DIVIDED BY LEAG. AVER.	E/G DIVIDED BY LEAG. AVER.
	FA	PO	A	DP	E		
SISLER	0	0	7	3	6	+30%	+31%
TERRY	2	5	5	3	0	+17%	−16%
FOXX	3	1	3	0	1	+ 6%	−23%
MIZE	2	2	2	1	2	− 2%	−11%
GREENBERG	1	2	2	0	1	+ 1%	− 2%
GEHRIG	0	2	1	1	2	−15%	−14%
MUSIAL	3	0	0	1	0	+ 7%	− 15%
BROUTHERS	1	1	0	2	2	+ 2%	+ 5%
ALLEN	0	0	0	0	2	−22%	+ 27%
MCCOVEY	0	0	1	0	5	−11%	+ 42%

an older player. For other infield positions, as noted in later chapters, the league average stats move dramatically over time. However, first base fielding statistics have not fluctuated much. The fielding percentage was about .974 before 1900, but it rose rapidly to .990 and has stayed there since 1915. Assists per game were only about .39 before 1900, in Dan Brouther's time, but also rose rapidly to .60 from 1915 to 1940. They rose slowly after that, peaking at .66 in Killebrew's time, and settling a bit since then. Errors per game also have not fluctuated much over the past ninety years, slowly dropping from .11 to about .07 now. The chart above compares assists and errors per game with the average of a player's time.

I also decided to look at the times a player led the league in a given category. The short list of candidates for all-time honors is reduced to nine players, and this selection process is detailed in chapter six. The results are shown above.

These numbers are somewhat helpful, and the assists are probably the best measure of individual ability, so I weighted them accordingly. I also looked at relative assists per game. My final defensive ranking, however, includes some subjective information from opinion polls, given the acute lack of help from the numbers.

4-Star First Basemen. George Sisler and Bill Terry had the reputation for being the best for the first half of baseball's history. Sisler led the league seven times in assists. Terry was a perennial leader in several categories. The problem I have with Sisler is that he also led the league a phenomenal six times in errors, and his errors per game were much worse than the average player of his day. That kind of performance is certainly not a 4-Star effort. Keith Hernandez, not a candidate for overall dream team, was the best on this side of 1950, as his twelve Gold Gloves attest. Ed Konetchy deserves note also, leading the league nine times in fielding percentage and five times in both putouts and assists. I am giving the fourth star to Terry for the solid stats which back up his reputation over time.

3-Star First Basemen. Sisler's tremendous assist record is far out in front of all others and clearly merits second place and a third star. Noncandidates like Gil Hodges, Vic Power, Don Mattingly and Fred Tenney truly distinguished themselves by defensive play, however.

2-Star First Basemen. Jimmy Foxx is in third place overall and gets a strong second star. I'm giving Stan Musial two stars too, since his fielding average and assists per game were nearly exceptional. Hank Greenberg and Johnny Mize take the next two slots, in that order, all above-average first sackers.

1-Star First Basemen. Lou Gehrig and Dan Brouthers had average stats.

0-Star First Basemen. Dick Allen and Willie McCovey were well below average.

SECOND BASE DEFENSIVE RANKINGS

Before we get to the numbers, we need to discuss this defensive ranking. Second base is considered the key to the infield, and is the key to defense.

In his interesting book on defense, *Nine Sides of the Diamond*, David Falkner writes of the qualifications of a great second baseman: "A second baseman needs to cover ground, and must be able to move to the left or right, to go back for balls over his head or in for balls slowly chopped. His hands must be soft enough to handle hot shots, quick enough to be able to separate the ball from the glove for double plays and relay throws. His feet need to be even quicker, in moving to work on double plays, precisely, perfectly."

Defensive Statistics: Second Base

PLAYER	FA	G	PO/G	A/G	E/G	DP/G	FR
LAJOIE	.963	2,035	5,496/2.7	6,262/3.1	451/.22	1,050/.52	370
E. COLLINS	.970	2,650	6,526/2.5	7,630/2.9	435/.16	1,215/.46	52
HORNSBY	.965	1,561	3,206/2.1	5,166/3.3	307/.20	893/.57	112
FRISCH	.974	1,762	4,348/2.5	6,026/3.4	280/.16	1,064/.60	139
GEHRINGER	.976	2,206	5,369/2.4	7,068/3.2	309/.14	1,444/.65	31
MORGAN	.981	2,527	5,742/2.3	6,967/2.8	244/.10	1,505/.60	205
GRICH	.984	1,765	4,217/2.4	5,381/3.1	156/.09	1,302/.74	97
SANDBERG	.990	1,666	3,280/2.0	5,443/3.3	92/.06	983/.59	144

Let's take a close look at the numbers. PO/G signifies put-outs and putouts per game, and so with assists, errors and double plays. I found the stats inadequate, but we have to live with them. The most useful, of course, are fielding percentage and assists per game. The former picks up errors, and the latter is the best individual measure of defensive performance. It helps us measure how many grounders per game the player got to, and is a good measure of range. Putouts per game is also useful, as it gets to the ability to go back on pop-ups or spear line drives. But since it also picks up force-outs at second (a relatively easy play), it is diluted. Of course, double plays are of great importance as well, although here again it's not an individual stat since it takes two good plays to make a double play. The chart above lists players according to the era in which they played, oldest first. I will discuss in chapter seven how I arrived at the short list of candidates for All-Time Dream Team second baseman.

The second basemen selected are spread out over all eras of baseball. Thus, the ability to directly compare defensive performance is severely hampered. Defensive stats are of some help, and we'll need to consider some opinion data, but this may be the toughest ranking we have come across so far.

As with other positions, I decided to look at the stats of the contemporaries of each player, those who primarily played at second base, who played at least five years at the position, and whose careers were wholly within the time period of the player being compared. The patterns were interesting. Fielding percentages rose from about .949 during Lajoie's time to about .983 today. They rose quickly, as fields and gloves improved after 1920.

Putouts per game, 2.3 during Lajoie's time, dipped a bit when the lively ball was introduced, but improved to 2.45 through the 1920s to 1940s as better gloves came about and double plays increased. The statistics dipped again during Morgan's time (2.1) as the sluggers moved the game more to the outfield. Assists per game, 2.9 for the Lajoie era, rose to 3.2 for Hornsby's time and dipped again to today's 2.7. Double plays rose rapidly between Lajoie's and Hornsby's time and have pretty much stayed constant since then. I then compared how far ahead each player's stats were against the average of their time.

The first column of data is the difference between the player's fielding percentage and that of the average of his contemporaries. The next columns compare the putouts, assists, and double plays per game with those of other players of the time, dividing one by the other.

4-Star Second Basemen. Well, the opinions over time have Napoleon Lajoie as an infielder of transcendent gracefulness, and the numbers back up that view. He led the league three times in assists, five times in putouts, and six times in double plays. He was an astounding 58 percent ahead of his time in double plays. Eddie Collins is a close second to Lajoie, and led the league during his years seven times in putouts, four times in assists, and five times in double plays. There are two noncandidates who defined the standard of play for their era: Bid McPhee, back in the late 1800s, led the league eight times in fielding percentage and in putouts, and eleven times in double plays; Bill Mazeroski is the best this side of 1950 with nine league-leading years in assists and eight in double plays.

3-Star Second Basemen. The new kids on the block, Bobby Grich, badly underrated during his time, and still active Ryne Sandberg both get three stars. Grich got only four gloves but was consistently among defensive leaders each year. Sandberg has collected nine Gold Gloves, and has led the league six times in assists. Charlie Gehringer led his league seven

Eddie Collins

times in assists, four times in double plays and three times in putouts. I'm not sure of the three stars here, since the jump from Lajoie and Collins is a significant one.

2-Star Second Basemen. Joe Morgan's assists were well

Percentage Comparison of Fielding Stats of Final Second Base Candidates Compared to the Average Player of the Time

PLAYER	FA MINUS LEAGUE AVER.	PO/G DIVIDED BY LEAGUE AVER.	A/G DIVIDED BY LEAGUE AVER.	DP/G DIVIDED BY LEAGUE AVER.
LAJOIE	+.014	+18%	+ 7%	+58%
E. COLLINS	+.015	+17%	+ 2%	+16%
GRICH	+.006	+16%	+15%	+23%
SANDBERG	+.008	+ 2%	+20%	+00%
GEHRINGER	+.010	– 1%	+ 7%	+11%
MORGAN	+.004	+10%	+10%	+ 1%
FRISCH	+.006	+ 3%	+ 6%	+ 7%
HORNSBY	–.003	–14%	+ 3%	+ 2%

above average. However, he was in good company during his era and so he led the league in assists only once (three times in putouts, and once in double plays). His five Gold Gloves attest to superb play, but the numbers don't seem to justify a third star, and the Gold Gloves are too often criticized to allow them to dominate our choice. The *Players' Choice* survey did not rate him as exceptional, so I must go with a very strong two stars. "The Fordham Flash," Frankie Frisch, was clearly above average, and led the league three times in fielding percentage and once in each of the other three categories. I spent a lot of time on defense because, as noted, second base carries a substantial defensive priority. The middle is where we stop runs.

1-Star Second Baseman. This may be a gift for Rogers Hornsby who had serious trouble with pop-ups. His otherwise average performance, however, slips him one star.

SHORTSTOP DEFENSIVE RANKINGS

The players listed on page 49 comprise the short list for the shortstop position. The method for selecting this list is detailed in chapter eight. Players are listed in chronological order, oldest era first. Note how fielding percentages improve over time while putouts, assists and errors decrease.

Shortstop Defensive Statistics

PLAYER	FA	G	PO/G	A/G	E/G	DP/G	FR
JENNINGS	922	899	2,390/2.7	3,147/3.5	470/.52	411/.46	150
WAGNER	.940	1,887	4,576/2.4	6,041/3.2	676/.36	766/.41	114
MARANVILLE	.952	2,153	5,139/2.4	7,354/3.4	631/.29	1,183/.55	177
BANCROFT	.944	1,873	4,623/2.5	6,561/3.5	660/.35	1,017/.54	200
CRONIN	.951	1,843	3,696/2.0	5,814/3.2	485/.26	1,165/.63	66
VAUGHAN	.951	1,485	2,995/2.0	4,780/3.2	397/.27	850/.57	−40
BOUDREAU	.973	1,539	3,132/2.0	4,760/3.1	223/.14	1,180/.77	136
BANKS	.969	1,125	2,087/1.9	3,441/3.1	174/.15	724/.64	3
APARICIO	.972	2,581	4,548/1.8	8,016/3.1	366/.14	1,553/.60	50
YOUNT	.964	1,479	2,588/1.7	4,794/3.2	272/.18	941/.64	14
O. SMITH	.979	2,322	3,962/1.7	7,821/3.4	258/.11	1,459/.63	238
RIPKEN	.978	1,885	3,083/1.6	5,780/3.1	197/.10	1,282/.68	38

As with second base, defensive ability is primary for short-stops. So, in order to evaluate the stats in context, I decided to look at the stats of the contemporaries of each player, as I did with second basemen. I looked only at players who primarily played at shortstop, who played at least five years at the position, and whose careers were wholly within the time period of the player being compared. I then compared how far ahead each player's stats were against the average of their time.

The players on page 50 are listed according to how I evaluate the degree to which they were ahead of their contemporaries. The first column of data is the difference between the player's fielding percentage and that of the average of his contemporaries. The next columns compare the putouts, assists, and double plays per game with those of other players of the time, dividing one by the other. I rate assists per game as the most important measure since they occur most often, although all four statistics are important.

4-Star Shortstops. Ozzie Smith is the best defensive shortstop ever. His thirteen consecutive Gold Gloves is phenome-

Percentage Comparison of Fielding Stats of Final Shortstop Candidates Compared to the Average Player of the Time

PLAYER	FA MINUS LEAGUE AVER.	PO/G DIVIDED BY LEAGUE AVER.	A/G DIVIDED BY LEAGUE AVER.	DP/G DIVIDED BY LEAGUE AVER.
O. SMITH	+ .014	+ 22%	**+ 34%**	+ 19%
APARICIO	+ .008	+ 33%	+ 14%	+ 22%
RIPKEN	+ .013	+ 17%	+ 22%	**+ 28%**
MARANVILLE	+ .011	+ 21%	+ 15%	+ 17%
JENNINGS	+ .005	**+ 29%**	+ 11%	**+ 31%**
WAGNER	**+ .023**	+ 14%	+ 1%	+ 17%
BANCROFT	+ .003	+ 26%	+ 18%	+ 15%
BOUDREAU	+ .015	+ 6%	+ 5%	+ 23%
YOUNT	+ .000	+ 26%	+ 18%	+ 25%
BANKS	+ .007	+ 20%	+ 14%	+ 12%
CRONIN	+ .002	+ 1%	+ 8%	+ 8%
VAUGHAN	+ .002	+ 1%	+ 8%	– 3%

nal. He led the league in assists nine of his first fourteen years, and assists are the best measure of a shortstop. He was way ahead of the average of his time, a phenomenal 34 percent. However, he has a lot of company. Louis Aparicio (nine Gold Gloves, eight times league leader in fielding percentage, seven times in assists) and Rabbit Maranville (who led the league in each category several times or more) clearly qualify for four stars. I can't figure out why Cal Ripken was overlooked for Gold Gloves before back-to-back wins in 1991 and 1992. He has led the league in assists, putouts or double plays nearly half the time. I'm giving him all four stars too.

3-Star Shortstops. Hughie Jennings, Honus Wagner and Dave Bancroft were exceptional shortstops. Many would give the fourth star to Wagner, and his .940 fielding percentage was astonishing for the turn-of-the-century conditions. But he did not lead the league enough in fielding categories during his career for the fourth star (putouts only twice, assists never, double plays four times, fielding percentage four

Third Basemen Defensive Statistics

PLAYER	FA	G	PO/G	A/G	E/G	DP/G	FR
J. COLLINS	.929	1,683	2,372/1.4	3,702/2.2	465/.28	225/.13	139
BAKER	.943	1,548	2,154/1.4	3,155/2.0	322/.21	259/.17	38
TRAYNOR	.947	1,863	2,289/1.2	3,521/1.8	324/.17	303/.16	36
LINDSTROM	.959	809	835/1.0	1,536/1.9	102/.13	135/.17	26
KELL	.969	1,692	1,825/1.1	3,303/2.0	166/.10	306/.18	-17
MATHEWS	.956	2,181	2,049/0.9	4,322/1.9	293/.13	369/.17	-15
ROBINSON	.971	2,870	2,697/0.9	6,205/2.2	263/.09	618/.22	151
SCHMIDT	.955	2,212	1,591/0.7	5,045/2.3	313/.14	450/.20	265
BRETT	.951	1,689	1,370/0.8	3,669/2.2	260/.15	306/.18	-17
BOGGS	.960	1,654	1,240/0.8	3,268/2.0	189/.11	327/.20	30

times). There is a noticeable break in the numbers after the first four players, so I draw a natural line at that point.

2-Star Shortstops. Lou Boudreau, Robin Yount and Ernie Banks were clearly well-above-average shortstops.

1-Star Shortstops. Joe Cronin and Arky Vaughan were known more for their bats.

THIRD BASE DEFENSIVE RANKINGS

Although the sabermetricians give a strong nod to Mike Schmidt, who was certainly no slouch at the hot corner with ten Gold Gloves to his credit, the memory of Brooks Robinson's great diving plays looms larger in the minds of fans. His sixteen Gold Gloves (the most ever) ring loud and clear of superstar defensive ability. Brooks could dive to either side and catch or knock down balls that one would think were impossible to get to. And he would do this game after game. His glove transcended those of all other fielders at third base and easily was the best of all time. He leads the pack in double plays per game and in lowest errors per game. Let's look at the numbers above. Players are listed chronologically, old-timers first.

While not as critical as with shortstop and second base, the evaluation of defensive ability is still very important for third base. So, in order to evaluate the stats in context, we again need to look at the stats of the contemporaries of each player. As with other positions, we looked only at players who primarily played at third, who played at least five years at the position, and whose careers were wholly within the time period of the player being compared. I then compared how far ahead each player's stats were against the average of their time.

The players on page 53 are listed according to how I evaluate the degree to which they were ahead of their contemporaries. As with other infield positions, we find the fielding percentage rising from .913 in Collins's time to about .950 in the twenties. Curiously, it only rises a few more points on average during the next seventy years. The hot corner only gets so cool!

Putouts and assists per game are subject to different forces; improved fields and gloves would raise them and the movement of the action to the outfield with the lively ball would lower them. On average they have declined over the years. Double plays per game rise until the post war era and then settle a bit. Obviously, we need to compare players in context of their times.

The first column of data is the difference between the

Brooks Robinson

Percentage Comparison of Fielding Stats of Final Third Base Candidates Compared to the Average Player of the Time

PLAYER	FA MINUS LEAGUE AVER.	PO/G DIVIDED BY LEAGUE AVER.	A/G DIVIDED BY LEAGUE AVER.	DP/G DIVIDED BY LEAGUE AVER.
B. ROBINSON	+.021	+11%	+21%	+31%
SCHMIDT	+.002	+1%	+25%	+25%
J. COLLINS	+.016	+14%	+9%	+7%
BAKER	+.003	+14%	+3%	+22%
BRETT	−.002	+11%	+20%	+10%
BOGGS	+.007	+5%	+8%	+21%
MATHEWS	+.006	+11%	+11%	+3%
KELL	+.015	+11%	+4%	−3%
LINDSTROM	+.009	−4%	0%	−4%
TRAYNOR	−.003	+15%	−1%	−7%

player's fielding percentage and that of the average of his contemporaries. The next columns compare the putouts, assists, and double plays per game with those of other players of the time, dividing one by the other. As with shortstops, the better measure for third basemen is assists per game, since they account for the majority of play chances. However, all categories are useful.

4-Star Third Baseman. It's clearly Brooks Robinson in the first defensive spot. No player has so clearly dominated this position, or any other position, as completely as has Brooks. He alone has four stars; no one else is in his class!

3-Star Third Basemen. It's close between Mike Schmidt and Jimmie Collins for second, with Collins's sure glove and good range against the best arm ever at third. However, assists are the best measure at third, so I give a good edge to Schmidt and his ten Gold Gloves.

2-Star Third Basemen. Frank Baker, George Brett (a Gold Glove), Wade Boggs and Eddie Mathews were above the average of their times.

1-Star Third Basemen. George Kell (close to a second star),

Catcher Defensive Statistics

PLAYER	FA	G	PO/G	A/G	E	PB	DP	FR
EWING	.931	636	3,301/5.2	1,017/1.6	322	NA	78	64
BRESNAHAN	.971	974	4,309/4.4	1,195/1.2	167	129	96	−51
SCHALK	.981	1,727	7,168/4.2	1,811/1.0	175	NA	226	46
HARTNETT	.984	1,793	7,292/4.1	1,254/.70	139	126	163	78
COCHRANE	.985	1,451	6,414/4.4	840/.58	111	87	104	17
DICKEY	.988	1,708	7,965/4.6	954/.59	108	76	137	16
FERRELL	.984	1,806	7,248/4.0	1,127/.62	135	NA	139	26
LOMBARDI	.979	1,544	5,694/3.7	845/.55	143	143	107	−3
BERRA	.989	1,699	8,738/5.1	798/.47	110	76	175	47
CAMPANELLA	.988	1,183	6,520/5.5	550/.46	85	54	82	25
BENCH	.990	1,744	9,260/5.3	850/.49	97	100	127	−36
CARTER	.991	2,056	11,832/5.8	1,210/.59	121	NA	150	53

Fred Lindstrom (who is he?) and Pie Traynor come up with average stats overall. I'm surprised about Pie. He had the great bat, and so played steady enough to accumulate some league-leading years in several categories, but when divided by games played, he is close to average in all categories except putouts per game.

CATCHERS DEFENSIVE RANKINGS

The short list of candidates for dream team catcher includes a dozen players. The method for selecting these twelve is set forth in chapter ten. The players are listed in chronological order, old-timers first.

As with the other positions, we need to compare players against the average of their times. The trouble with catchers is that the stats are nearly useless, as is also the case at first base. The only stats which help are fielding percentage, to measure sureness of glove, and assists per game, which picks up bunt action and steal attempts. Double plays are of some use, although these stats pick up mainly plays at the plate after a fly out, and such plays mainly rely on the accuracy and speed of the throw to the plate. Putouts would be helpful if they didn't cram all the strikeouts into this stat, rendering it

Percentage Comparison of Fielding Stats of Final Catcher Candidates Compared to the Average Player of the Time

PLAYER	FA MINUS LEAGUE AVER.	A/G DIVIDED BY LEAGUE AVER.
Buck EWING	+.018%	+15.7%
Gary CARTER	+.007%	+24.9%
Gabby HARTNETT	+.006%	+19.9%
Rick FERRELL	+.005%	+21.1%
Bill DICKEY	+.009%	+ 8.4%
Johnny BENCH	+.006%	+ 5.4%
Yogi BERRA	+.006%	+ 3.9%
Ray SCHALK	+.009%	+ 2.0%
Roy CAMPANELLA	+.005%	+ 2.9%
Ernie LOMBARDI	000	+ 6.2%
Mickey COCHRANE	+.007%	– 0.7%
Roger BRESNAHAN	+.003%	– 7.8%

useless. As with the other positions, I decided to look only at players who primarily played at catcher, who played at least five years at the position, and whose careers were wholly within the time period of the player being compared. I then compared how far ahead each player's stats were against the average of their time.

Fielding averages increased dramatically after 1900, and five points a decade after that. Putouts per game and especially assists per game were higher during the days of slapstick ball, although the modern era sees a slight increase as "Billy Ball" speed seems to be returning to the game a bit.

4-Star Catchers. Number one goes to Buck Ewing. His fielding percentage, putouts per game and assists per game were the best, overall, of the lot. His fielding percentage is eighteen points over the average of the times. His assists per game of 1.6 is among the highest ever, way ahead of his contemporaries (although it is understood that catchers got a lot more bunt action in the old days). I noted at the outset that assists were probably the best available statistical measure of catchers. Ewing has the highest sabermetric statistic for fielding runs. He caught only 636 games, but played another 700 games divided among all other positions (he played them all but pitcher). He played 253 games at first base and 235 in the outfield. For second place I must go with Gary Carter. I don't have a clue how Johnny Bench got ten Gold Gloves and Carter got only three. Bench led the league in fielding, putouts, assists and double plays only once each, while Carter led it two times in fielding percentage, eight times in putouts, five times in assists, and five times in double plays. Gabby Hartnett also was great in all categories and gets third place.

3-Star Catchers. Johnny Bench had a fearsome arm, one of the best ever, and it is a sure thing that runners were afraid of him, explaining partially the relatively low assists. His Gold Gloves, while perhaps a bit overrated, must speak loudly here since the stats for the catcher position are so poor. They certainly earn him three stars and fourth place. Yogi Berra was an exceptional catcher, and got the second most double plays and tenth most putouts ever. Roy Campanella is a very close sixth, followed by Bill Dickey. Ray Schalk had a great glove, the most double plays ever, and the second most assists over a long career. He was the first catcher to back up first and third.

2-Star Catchers. Rick Ferrell had an exceptional rate of assists and above-average performance in other areas. He is followed by Mickey Cochrane and Ernie Lombardi as above-average catchers.

1-Star Catcher. A gift for Roger Bresnahan, who had a fair glove.

SUMMARY: BEST DEFENSE BY DREAM TEAM CANDIDATES

Again I remind the reader that these ratings cover only the candidates for the dream team, not all players. If this were an all-time defensive team, the top positions would probably include Keith Hernandez at first base and Bill Mazerowski at second base, with either Richie Ashburn or Max Carey in the outfield.

FIRST BASE	Bill Terry ****
	George Sisler ***
SECOND BASE	Napoleon Lajoie ****
	Eddie Collins ****
THIRD BASE	Brooks Robinson ****
	Mike Schmidt ***
SHORTSTOP	Ozzie Smith ****
	Louis Aparicio ****
CATCHER	Buck Ewing ****
	Gary Carter ****
OUTFIELD	Willie Mays ****
	Tris Speaker ****
	Joe DiMaggio ***
	Roberto Clemente ***

Chapter Four

The Opinions

Over all of baseball's history, writers, fans and other commentators have regularly and happily stepped forward to deliver their own opinions as to who were the best ballplayers ever.

In 1950, sportswriter and nationally known baseball personality Christy Walsh had the great idea to have the "All-America Board of Baseball" select the dream team for the first fifty years of baseball. In doing so, he provided an enormously valuable benchmark of opinion regarding players in the first half-century. This board was chaired by Hall of Famer Connie Mack, a catcher in the late 1800s, and ultimately the manager and owner of the Philadelphia Athletics for fifty years. The method used for the team was to mail a survey to five hundred sportswriters. The results were tallied, and the top nominees were then considered by the thirteen-member board who ultimately voted for the All-America All-Time Team. The results of both the original survey and the final selection are reported in *Baseball's Greatest Lineup* and are included herein. While it remains a most important work, the survey inexplicably excluded players from before 1900.

The next major opinion poll was undertaken by the Baseball Writers Association of America, in honor of baseball's centennial in 1969. Dick Young, New York's dean of modern-day sportswriters and president of the BBWAA, headed up a committee of sportswriters who chose the team. Fans from every major league city nominated players, and all Hall of Famers were also included. The committee also chose a second list from all living players to add interest to the process.

The winners were listed in the August 2, 1969, edition of *The Sporting News*.

Another important survey was conducted in 1987 by Eugene and Roger McCaffrey. Their method was to mail a questionnaire to five thousand baseball players and coaches, covering all time periods since 1900. Unfortunately, only 645 surveys were returned, but the results are most useful and were reported in their book *Players' Choice*. This "must read" book goes on to rate players in numerous interesting categories, such as best fastball, best curve, most inspirational, etc.

A fourth major opinion survey, of sorts, is the annual balloting of the Baseball Writers Association of America in the Most Valuable Player Award given each year in both leagues. There is a compelling argument that the best opinions are those made at the same time of play, and MVP votes are cast by expert observers each year for that year. The vote tally for each player in each year since 1923 is reported in Thorn and Palmer's *Total Baseball*. I have reported here the number of times each great player received the award, and furthermore how often they were listed in the top-five and top-ten vote totals. Bill James in his *Historical Baseball Abstract* firmly advocates the value of MVP as an opinion poll. He has developed a statistic which takes the portion of votes received by a player from the total votes available, and adds up the total of these percentages over a player's career. He calls it the MVP "share."

The results of these and other surveys are reported in the following table. What is readily apparent is the extent to which the various opinions differ, with some definite exceptions.

Beyond the major opinion surveys already mentioned, and I rely most heavily upon the four cited, are several other sources of opinion. The All-America Board selection committee is not, in my judgment, as powerful as the underlying survey of five hundred writers which they conducted. Five hundred sportswriters give a broader view than thirteen "experts." However, the Board's views are important, and are listed. Christy Walsh's book also presents the individual choices of Connie Mack, as well as a rebuttal by famed sports-

THE OPINIONS AND CHOICES OF WRITERS,

THE OPINIONS FROM BASEBALL'S FIRST FIFTY YEARS

	ALL-AMERICA BOARD SURVEY OF 500 WRITERS	ALL-AMERICA BOARD SELECTION COMMITTEE	CONNIE MACK	FRED LIEB
1B	GEHRIG SISLER TERRY	SISLER	GEHRIG	GEHRIG
2B	GEHRINGER HORNSBY E. COLLINS	E. COLLINS	E. COLLINS	LAJOIE E. COLLINS
SS	WAGNER MARION CRONIN	WAGNER	WAGNER	WAGNER
3B	TRAYNOR J. COLLINS BAKER	TRAYNOR	J. COLLINS	TRAYNOR
OF	RUTH COBB SPEAKER TIE DIMAGGIO TIE JACKSON WILLIAMS OTT	RUTH COBB SPEAKER DIMAGGIO JACKSON	RUTH COBB SPEAKER	RUTH COBB SPEAKER
C	COCHRANE DICKEY HARTNETT	DICKEY COCHRANE	COCHRANE DICKEY	BRESNAHAN KLING
HON. MEN		DIMAGGIO FRISCH	DIMAGGIO FRISCH	DIMAGGIO HORNSBY
P	JOHNSON MATHEWSON GROVE ALEXANDER YOUNG HUBBELL WADDELL WALSH	JOHNSON MATHEWSON YOUNG ALEXANDER GROVE HUBBELL	MATHEWSON JOHNSON YOUNG ALEXANDER GROVE HUBBELL	JOHNSON MATHEWSON YOUNG ALEXANDER GROVE HUBBELL WADDELL FELLER

PLAYERS AND COACHES

POS	PLAYERS' CHOICE SURVEY OF 645 PLAYERS (1987)	% OF VOTES	MVP AWARDS 1922-1992 BBWAA				1969 CENTENNIAL BBWAA ALL-TIME TEAM	
			MVP VOTES	# WINS	TOP 5	TOP 10		
1B	GEHRIG	36.0%	MUSIAL	3	9	13	GEHRIG	
	MUSIAL	7.6%	GEHRIG	2	8	9	SISLER	
	FOXX	6.1%	FOXX	3	6	6	MUSIAL	
2B	GEHRINGER	17.8%	MORGAN	3	4	5	HORNSBY	
	HORNSBY	16.8%	HORNSBY	3	4	4	GEHRINGER	
	ROBINSON	8.8%	E. COLLINS	1	5	6	E. COLLINS	
SS	WAGNER	16.4%	BANKS	2	3	5	WAGNER	
	APARICIO	13.8%	BOUDREAU	1	3	5	CRONIN	
	BANKS	8.3%					BANKS	
3B	B. ROBINSON	39.2%	SCHMIDT	3	5	8	TRAYNOR	
	TRAYNOR	14.8%	B. ROBINSON	1	5	7	B. ROBINSON	
	SCHMIDT	7.1%	BRETT	1	4	5	J. ROBINSON	
OF	MAYS	12.9%	MANTLE	3	9	9	RUTH	
	DIMAGGIO	12.9%	DIMAGGIO	3	7	10	COBB	
	RUTH	12.2%	MAYS	2	9	12	DIMAGGIO	
	WILLIAMS	12.2%	WILLIAMS	2	9	12	WILLIAMS	
	MANTLE	8.0%	ROBINSON	2	7	12	SPEAKER	
	AARON	7.1%	AARON	1	8	13	MAYS	
	MUSIAL	6.2%	RICE	1	6	6		
	COBB	5.8%	PARKER	1	6	6		
	CLEMENTE	2.7%	WANER	1	5	7		
C	BENCH	23.9%	BERRA	2	7	7	COCHRANE	
	DICKEY	21.8%	BENCH	2	4	4	DICKEY	
	BERRA	15.2%	COCHRANE	2	3	4	CAMPANELLA	
	COCHRANE	11.8%	CAMPANELLA	3	2	3		
	CAMPANELLA	10.2%	HARTNETT	1	2	2		

RHP		LHP		P				RHP	LHP
JOHNSON	17.5%	KOUFAX	31.0%	HUBBELL	2	3	4	JOHNSON	GROVE
FELLER	16.9%	GROVE	19.8%	NEWHOUSER	2	3	3	MATHEWSON	KOUFAX
GIBSON	13.2%	SPAHN	15.3%	FELLER	0	5	7	YOUNG	HUBBELL
SEAVER	6.3%	CARLTON	11.0%	KOUFAX	1	3	3		
DEAN	4.7%	HUBBELL	8.2%	SPAHN	0	4	4		
YOUNG	4.4%	FORD	6.5%	GROVE	1	2	3		
MATHEWSON	4.0%	GOMEZ	3.0%	GIBSON	1	2	2		

MORE OPINIONS AND CHOICES

	MAURY ALLEN'S 1981 TOP 100 PLAYERS	THORN AND PALMER *TOTAL BASEBALL* RATING	FABER'S RATINGS 1985	*SPORT MAGAZINE* 1977 ALL-TIME ALL-STARS	1992 *SPORTS ILLUSTRATED* DREAM TEAM
1B	GEHRIG	GEHRIG	GEHRIG	GEHRIG	GEHRIG
	SISLER	FOXX	FOXX		
	GREENBERG	CONNOR	TERRY		
2B	HORNSBY	LAJOIE	LAJOIE	HORNSBY	J. ROBINSON
	J. ROBINSON	HORNSBY	E. COLLINS		
	CAREW	E. COLLINS	DOERR		
SS	WAGNER	WAGNER	WAGNER	WAGNER	WAGNER
	BANKS	DAHLEN	BANKS		
		WALLACE	WALLACE		
3B	B. ROBINSON	SCHMIDT	SANTO	B. ROBINSON	SCHMIDT
	CRONIN	MATHEWS	B. ROBINSON		
	BRETT	BRETT	SCHMIDT		
OF	MAYS	RUTH	RUTH	COBB	RUTH
	AARON	COBB	COBB	MAYS	COBB
	RUTH	WILLIAMS	SPEAKER	WILLIAMS	MAYS
	WILLIAMS	AARON	MAYS	RUTH (DH)	
	MUSIAL	SPEAKER	WILLIAMS		
	DIMAGGIO	MAYS	AARON		
	COBB	MUSIAL	SIMMONS		
	CLEMENTE	F. ROBINSON	MUSIAL		
	SPEAKER	MANTLE	MANTLE		
	OTT	OTT	DIMAGGIO		
C	DICKEY	HARTNETT	BERRA	DICKEY	COCHRANE
	BERRA	DICKEY	DICKEY		
	COCHRANE	BERRA	BENCH		
P	JOHNSON	JOHNSON	NOT RATED	JOHNSON	MATHEWSON
	MATHEWSON	YOUNG		FORD	SPAHN
	ALEXANDER	ALEXANDER			ECKERSLEY
	GROVE	NICHOLS			
	KOUFAX	MATHEWSON			
	FELLER	GROVE			
	DEAN	CLARKSON			
	SPAHN	SEAVER			
	FORD	GIBSON			
	HUBBELL	SPAHN			

		BILL JAMES'S PICKS	BABE RUTH'S PICKS	TY COBB'S PICKS	WALTER JOHNSON'S PICKS	NAP LAJOIE'S PICKS
1B		GEHRIG	CHASE	SISLER	CHASE	CHASE
		FOXX				
		MCCOVEY				
2B		E. COLLINS	LAJOIE	LAJOIE	LAJOIE	HORNSBY
		MORGAN				
		LAJOIE				
SS		WAGNER	WAGNER	WAGNER	WAGNER	WAGNER
		APPLING				
		BANKS				
3B		SCHMIDT	J. COLLINS	WEAVER	J. COLLINS	BRADLEY
		MATHEWS				
		B. ROBINSON				
OF		RUTH	X	RUTH	COBB	COBB
		MUSIAL	COBB	SPEAKER	SPEAKER	BEAUMONT
		AARON	SPEAKER	JACKSON	RUTH	MCALEER
		COBB				
		MAYS				
		DIMAGGIO				
		ROSE				
		SPEAKER				
C		BERRA	SCHALK	COCHRANE	DICKEY	COCHRANE
		BENCH			KLING	
		COCHRANE				
P		GROVE	JOHNSON	JOHNSON	ALEXANDER	MATHEWSON
		SPAHN	MATHEWSON	ALEXANDER		JOHNSON
		JOHNSON	ALEXANDER	PLANK		
		FORD	PENNOCK			
		MATHEWSON				
		FELLER				

writer and author Fred Lieb. I present all four lists in the first table.

The next table presents the *Players' Choice*, the MVP voting, and the Centennial Team picks.

The third and fourth tables present the picks from a number of other books or magazines on the subject. Thorn and Palmer's are strictly statistical picks, based on sabermetric offensive and defensive games won statistics.

Finally, we hear from the players themselves as reported in their autobiographies or from interviews. The work of Lawrence Ritter in his fabulous book of interviews with old-time players, *The Glory of Their Times*, is a priceless contribution to the memory of the game.

PLAYERS AND OTHERS SPEAK OUT

Honus Wagner. Ed Barrow, who managed Babe Ruth and saw a lot of Ty Cobb said in *The Glory of Their Times*, "If I had a choice of all men who have played baseball, the first man I would select is Honus Wagner." John McGraw, the great manager of the Giants, echoed, "I consider Wagner not only as the number one shortstop, but had he played in any other position except pitcher, he would have been equally as great at the other seven positions."

"Honus Wagner didn't look like a shortstop, you know. He had those big shoulders and those bowed legs, and he didn't seem to field balls the way we did. He just ate the ball up with his big hands, like a scoop shovel, and when he threw it to first base you'd see pebbles and dirt and everything else flying along there with the ball. It was quite a sight! The greatest shortstop ever. The greatest anything ever," said Tommy Leach, who played third base with Wagner.

And said teammate Sam Crawford, "He could play any position except pitcher and easily be the best in the league at it. He was a wonderful fielder, terrific arm, very quick, all over the place grabbing sure hits and turning them into outs . . . a good team man too, and the sweetest disposition in the world. The greatest ballplayer who ever lived in my book."

Napoleon Lajoie. Tommy Leach said of Nap Lajoie, "What a ballplayer that man was. Every play he made he executed so gracefully that it looked like it was the easiest thing in the world. He was a pleasure to play against, too, always laughing and joking. Even when the son of a gun was blocking the base he was smiling and kidding. You just had to like this guy."

Fred Lieb, the dean of sportswriters from 1911 to 1933, paid a great tribute to Nap in a comparison with the immortal Honus Wagner. Lieb said in *Baseball As I Have Known It*, "Older boys and men in our neighborhood used to argue by the hour: Who is greater, Honus or King Larry (Lajoie)? As I grew older and saw them consistently, I began to lean towards Wagner."

Buck Ewing. Bill James in his *Historical Baseball Abstract* found two respected editors of baseball guides, in 1919 and in 1930, who spoke of Buck Ewing, who played in the 1880s. The *Reach Guide* said, "The three greatest players up to that time were Ty Cobb, Honus Wagner and Buck Ewing. It is a difficult task to select one player as superior to all the rest, though we have always been inclined to consider catcher/manager Buck Ewing in his prime as the greatest player of the game from the standpoint of supreme excellence in all departments." Writer Sam Crane said in a 1912 article for the *New York Journal*, "Ewing was as near to being free of any weakness as a ballplayer as the great Ty Cobb is today."

Ty Cobb. "Ty Cobb didn't have a sense of humor, see. Especially, he could never laugh at himself. Consequently, he took a lot of things the wrong way. He had such a rotten disposition, that an innocent wisecrack would become cause for a fistfight if Ty was involved. It was too bad. He was one of the greatest players who ever lived, and yet he had so few friends. I always felt sorry for him," said Davy Jones, Cobb's teammate and "friend."

Rube Waddell. "Rube Waddell was just a big kid, you know. He'd pitch one day and we wouldn't see him for three or four days after that. He'd just disappear, go fishing or something, or be off playing ball with a bunch of twelve-year-olds in an empty lot somewhere. You couldn't control him. Baseball was just a game to Rube," said the great Sam Crawford, who broke in with Rube, in *The Glory of Their Times*.

Walter Johnson. Sam Crawford said of teammate Walter Johnson, "He had such an easy motion it looked like he was just playing catch. That's what threw you off. He threw so nice and easy, and then *swoosh*, the ball was by you. Walter was a wonderful person too, you know. He was always afraid he might hit somebody with that fastball. A wonderful man in every way. Warm and friendly, and wouldn't hurt a soul. Easily the greatest pitcher I ever saw."

Lefty Grove said in *Baseball When the Grass Was Real*, "Walter Johnson? I used to go home to watch that bugger pitch. We idolized that guy. Just sat there and watched him pitch. Down around the knees—whoosh! One after another. I haven't seen any one come close to as fast as he was."

Jimmy Austin played against Walter Johnson and said in *The Glory of Their Times*, "Lefty Grove was fast, and Sandy Koufax too. But you should have seen Walter Johnson. On a cloudy day you couldn't see the ball half the time, it came in so fast. That's the honest to God truth. But I'd still rather bat against Walter, so careful, he was scared stiff he'd hit somebody."

Lefty Grove. Wes Ferrell played with Lefty Grove and told Donald Honig in *Baseball When the Grass Was Real*, "He was my idol. Lefty Grove, fastest pitcher I ever saw. He'd throw that ball in there and you'd just wonder where it went to. It would just *zing!* and disappear. You can believe he was that fast because that's all he threw. He didn't start throwing breaking stuff until later in his career." Hall of Famer Charlie Gehringer echoed, "Grove's fastball wasn't that alive. It carried a little but never did anything tricky. But it was so fast that by the time you'd made up your mind whether it would be a strike or a ball, it just wasn't there anymore. It's hard to believe that anyone could throw faster than Lefty Grove."

Cochrane/Dickey. Charlie Gehringer also said of the Cochrane/Dickey debate, "Dickey could throw a little better. Cochrane was probably a better all-around guy; he could run faster, he could do more with the bat, he could do more things to beat you. He didn't have quite the power that Dickey did, though."

Satchel Paige. Cool Papa Bell was a Negro League star who made the Hall of Fame. He told *Baseball When the Grass Was Real*, "Satchel Paige was the fastest . . . I've seen Walter Johnson, Dizzy Dean, Bob Feller, Lefty Grove, all of them. All he threw for years was that fastball. It would be by you before you could turn. He could throw that ball right by your knees all day."

Willie Mays. Old-timer Al Bridwell played in 1905 and saw the best, but said in *The Glory of Their Times*, "Take Willie Mays. I've seen Speaker, Cobb, Hooper—oh, all the great outfielders—but I've never seen anyone who was any better than Willie Mays. . . . (he) can throw, field, hit, run, anything. He can work a pitcher into losing a ball game any time he gets on base." Harry Hooper also played at the turn of the century and agreed, "That Willie Mays. . . . You can go back as far as you want and name the great ones—Tris Speaker, Eddie Roush, Max Carey, Earle Combs, Joe DiMaggio. I don't care who you name, Mays is just as good, maybe better. He's a throwback to the old days. A guy who can do everything, and play like he loves it."

Said teammate and Hall of Famer Monte Irvin in Donald Honig's *Baseball Between the Lines*, "I think anybody who saw him will say that Mays was the greatest player who ever lived. He could do everything. I don't think there was ever a center fielder, Speaker, DiMaggio, Moore, or anyone else who was better than Willie in going and getting a ball. He would play shallow catching line drives, and at the same time you couldn't hit anything over his head. At the crack of a bat he was gone, and an arm like a cannon."

Joe Gordon, DiMaggio's teammate, was asked to compare DiMaggio and Mays, reported Charles Einstein in *The Fireside Book Of Baseball*. Gordon said flat out, "You are not going to like this, but the greatest player I ever saw is Willie Mays."

Ted Williams. Bob Feller said in *Baseball When the Grass Was Real*, "Ted Williams? Nobody had his number. He was the best hitter I ever pitched to."

Tris Speaker. Smoky Joe Wood roomed with Tris Speaker, and said in *The Glory of Their Times*, "Speaker played a real shallow center field and he had that terrific instinct—at the crack of the bat he'd be off with his back to the infield, and then he'd turn and glance over his shoulder at the last minute and catch the ball so easy like there was nothing to it. Nobody else was even in the same league with him."

Teammate and Hall of Famer Joe Sewell told *Legends of Baseball*, "I played with Tris for seven years as an outfielder.

I've seen Joe DiMaggio and I've seen Willie Mays . . . and all the rest. Tris Speaker is the best center fielder I've seen."

Eddie Collins. Connie Mack said of Eddie Collins in *Baseball's Greatest Lineup*, "No one could pick a better man for second base than Eddie Collins. He had everything. He had fighting spirit, he could hit, he could run the bases, and he was smart. He was daring too, but never reckless."

Babe Ruth. The views on Babe Ruth's fielding seem mixed. Rube Bressler told *The Glory of Their Times*, "One of the greatest pitchers of all time, and then he became a great judge of a fly ball, never threw to the wrong base, terrific arm. . . . He was a damn animal. He had that instinct. They know when it's going to rain, things like that. Nature, that was Ruth." In the same book, however, Harry Hooper, who played outfield with Ruth, said, "Well, Ruth might have been a natural as a pitcher and as a hitter, but he sure wasn't a born outfielder."

Well, Ruth could certainly hit. As also quoted in *The Glory of Their Times*, teammate Sam Jones said, "Babe Ruth could hit a ball so hard, and so far that it was sometimes impossible to believe your eyes. We used to absolutely marvel at his hits. Tremendous wallops. You can't imagine the balls that he hit." And Jimmy Austin echoed, "The Babe was always friendly, a real nice guy who'd go out of his way anytime to do you a favor, always time for a wisecrack or a laugh, a heart as big as a watermelon and made out of pure gold. I guess when you talk about the greatest baseball player ever it has to be either the Babe, Ty Cobb or Honus Wagner . . . they could beat you in so many ways."

Lou Gehrig. Jimmy Austin said of Lou Gehrig in *The Glory of Their Times*, "One of the nicest fellows that ever lived. He never really got the publicity he deserved. A very serious-minded fellow, very modest and easy to get along with, always every inch a gentleman."

Joe DiMaggio. Hank Greenberg said in *The Glory of Their Times*, "Everybody remembers Willie Mays's catch off Vic Wertz in the 1954 World Series, but few remember an even greater catch Joe DiMaggio made off me in 1939. I hit a tremendous line drive one day in Yankee Stadium that went at least 450 feet to deepest center field. Joe turned and raced towards the bleachers with his back to the plate; still running

Lou Gehrig and Babe Ruth

at full speed, without turning around or looking back, he stuck up his glove and the ball landed in it. Sheer instinct!"

Mickey Mantle. Donald Honig wrote in *Baseball America*, "I tell you, right handed he could drive the ball as far as Foxx, and left handed as far as Ruth. And he had running speed like you never saw. And an arm like a cannon. And he had that charisma, he had that too!"

A CONSENSUS OF OPINION

The attempt to rank players by aggregating the various opinion polls is most difficult, particularly since the polls and surveys were done over different times and early efforts could not consider later players. As noted earlier, the opinion section will be weighted most heavily for the four major surveys (1950 All-America Board, 1969 Centennial selection, *Players' Choice* and MVP voting). I will then consider secondarily the various individual opinions expressed by others such as Maury Allen, sports magazines and the players. The statistical opinions of James, Thorn and Faber will not be heavily considered since this evaluation is meant to capture subjective assessments.

While I will rank players individually, there are clear patterns to the polls and surveys I have presented, and use of a **Star** system, as done for offense and defense, will help to distinguish the favorites from the rest. I will award **4 Stars** for those who are clear and consistent favorites for all-time first team honors. **3 Stars** will go to those who are named for first team all-time honor on multiple polls, but are not clear favorites since they are in close competition with another player. **2 Stars** go to those not regularly named, but who have been mentioned at least once. This rating also is used for those who have been clearly surpassed by a later player and now get only runner-up honors. **1 Star** will cause me to closely review how they ever got on my short list!

Outfield

The candidates selected will be only those who appear as one of the top three choices on the various surveys.

4 Stars. Babe Ruth is on them all, and is the clear consensus choice for first team, number-one ranking. Ty Cobb was everybody's choice for the first fifty years, after Ruth of course. However, Cobb's stock has dropped a bit since then. He made the Centennial Team, but was a disappointing eighth in the *Players' Choice* poll, and his MVP recognition was curious indeed. Cobb won the first MVP award ever given in 1911 at the age of twenty-six, in the midst of his prime. However, he was most surprisingly overlooked in each of the next three MVP years, coming in eighth, twentieth and fourteenth, another curiosity. The award was not given again until 1922, near the end of his career. He was not in the top three in Maury Allen's survey, nor in Bill James's measures (which James said involved some subjectivity). It's close, but Cobb is still consistently regarded as one of the top three outfielders of all time, and he merits the fourth star. Willie Mays and Ted Williams could not have been considered for the 1950 poll, but they were both in the top three in the *Players' Choice* survey and in MVP voting, although neither made the top three in the Centennial vote (they both made the top six). Mays was included in the Maury Allen, *Sports Illustrated* and *Sport Magazine* top three, and was repeatedly mentioned by the players in the various interviews reported. However, the Centennial vote overlooked Willie, curiously, and that cost him a fourth star. Ted's defense kept him off too many top choices for a fourth star. DiMaggio was overlooked in 1950 and by a few other polls, so he also misses a fourth star.

3 Stars. Willie Mays narrowly missed a fourth star. The Centennial team did not have him in the top three, but he was in everything else and gets a third star and a third-place nod in the opinion category. Willie had the third highest MVP vote percentage during his career, behind only Stan Musial and Ted Williams. Joe DiMaggio is next, having been named in the *Players' Choice*, Centennial Team and MVP voting. However, he was overlooked, except in a "utility" role in the 1950 poll, at the end of his career, and was not selected by Allen, *Sport Magazine*, or even fellow Yankee Babe Ruth (or in Cobb's 1960 picks). So, "Joltin' Joe" will take fourth place and only three stars. Ted Williams was named in the *Sport Magazine* choice and the *Players' Choice* survey, and was fourth in the Centennial and Maury Allen's selections. He also had the second highest MVP vote percentage. It was close but I could only give a third star to Ted.

2 Stars. Tris Speaker was third man on all dream teams during the first fifty years, but has had a long fall since then and clearly lost his slot to the likes of Willie Mays. He is now only a runner-up in contemporary polls, and my rules give that only two stars. I think it's because his fame was mainly defensive, and that type of fame is the first to go. I'm amazed at how Mickey Mantle, widely renowned as one of the best players ever, is so rarely mentioned for all-time, all-star out-field teams. He was in the top three in none of our polls, except for his regularly high votes in the MVP voting (fourth highest MVP percentage of all time). Hank Aaron was listed sixth by the players poll and in the MVP list, and is named by Maury Allen. Stan Musial, Frank Robinson, Roberto Clemente and Mel Ott have all been mentioned, and take the final four slots in that order.

1 Star. Rickey Henderson and Darryl Strawberry have been named on no polls I'm aware of, and I'm not surprised about Darryl. Rickey, however, has always been underrated in my judgment.

First Base

4 Stars. Lou Gehrig is at the top on nearly every list. He stands alone on this one. No one else is close!

3 Stars. Let's face it. Defense was more important to base-ball in the old days than it is now. That's why the All-America Board overruled their own survey to go with George Sisler over Gehrig. (That's also what happened to Speaker.) Well, my dream team is one for all ages, and even though Sisler has been largely ignored since 1950, I have to go with his strong showing then and give him second place. The Centennial Team also gave him a second place. Stan Musial is first in MVP votes (some for outfield play), second in the *Players' Choice*, and third on Centennial, so he gets third place here. Jimmy Foxx also got 3-Star reviews with three MVPs (Gehrig only won two) and a decent showing in the players' poll.

2 Stars. I have to drop it down a notch for Bill Terry, who along with Hank Greenberg has gotten only honorable mentions.

1 Star. Johnny Mize, Dan Brouthers, Dick Allen and Willie McCovey have not been mentioned anywhere on these lists.

Second Base

4 Stars. My rules call for a clear and consistent consensus. There wasn't one here, so no one gets four stars.

3 Stars. First place goes to Charlie Gehringer. Too many others were named numero uno to give him a fourth star, but "The Mechanical Man" won both the 1950 writers' survey and the *Players' Choice* poll. Rogers Hornsby was second to Gehringer in both of those polls, but got top honors from the Centennial vote as well as from *Sport Magazine*, Maury Allen and MVP voting. Eddie Collins is a close third. He was third in the 1950 writers' poll, but somewhat curiously won the 1950 All-America Board selection committee vote. He also got Cobb's nod. Nap Lajoie was first with Lieb, Ruth and Walter Johnson. Joe Morgan hasn't been named as number one, but has done the best in MVP voting.

2 Stars. Frankie Frisch got an honorable mention from the 1950 All-America Board selection committee.

Shortstop

4 Stars. As clear as with Babe Ruth and Walter Johnson is Honus Wagner's claim to sole possession of all four stars in the views of fans over all of baseball's history.

3 Stars. My rules require some top votes for three stars, and no one else got any. Ernie Banks's two MVPs is not enough.

2 Stars. Not so clear. I'll give second place to Ernie Banks, who is ahead in MVP voting, and was second on Allen's list and third in the players' poll. Marty Marion was second in the 1950 writers' vote, but not heard from since then. Joe Cronin placed second in the Centennial vote and third with the 1950 writers. Lou Aparicio was second in the players' poll, but not otherwise listed. Lou Boudreau and Luke Appling also picked up some high votes in a poll or two.

1 Star. Ozzie Smith and Cal Ripken are still active, but will soon begin their march upward, especially Ripken. Rabbit Maranville, Dave Bancroft, Hughie Jennings and Arky Vaughan are not on any lists.

Third Base

4 Stars. Pie Traynor must squeak out a fourth star since he won the 1950 vote and the Centennial vote. However, it's by no means unanimous, with Brooks Robinson close behind.

3 Stars. It looks like Brooks Robinson gets a close second place in the opinion category. He won the *Players' Choice* survey, as well as Maury Allen's and *Sport Magazine*'s first pick. He was second to Traynor in the Centennial vote. Mike Schmidt, still playing at the time of the players' poll, still picked up a third there, and is the clear choice in MVP voting. Fourth place goes to Jimmy Collins, who was picked by Connie Mack, Babe Ruth and Walter Johnson, and this is enough for three stars.

2 Stars. George Brett got an MVP, and "top five" votes four times. Eddie Mathews was mentioned by Maury Allen.

1 Star. Home Run Baker was not on any lists. Neither were Wade Boggs, George Kell or Fred Lindstrom.

Catcher

4 Stars. Again, by my star rules, I have no clear and consistent winner here. No four stars can be awarded.

3 Stars. I have got to go with Mickey Cochrane for first ranking in a close one. He received the writers' vote in the All-America Board selection in 1950, and also won the Centennial vote. Bill Dickey won the vote of the All-America Board selection committee and got a very close second to Bench in the 1985 *Players' Choice* poll, and to Cochrane in the Centennial vote. He got the pick from Cobb, Allen, *Sport Magazine* and Walter Johnson. Johnny Bench won the players' poll, and is second in MVP placing, so he earned third place here. Yogi Berra is ahead in MVP voting, and got third in the *Players' Choice* survey. Buck Ewing was first in opinions expressed prior to 1925, but was forgotten after that.

2 Stars. Gabby Hartnett and Roger Bresnahan received only honorable mention votes.

Pitchers

The tables in this chapter do not include what is probably the best poll for pitchers in the last fifty years: the voting for the Cy Young Award, which began in 1956. Only five players have dominated the votes over its thirty-six-year history. Following are their names and, in parentheses, the number of Cy Young awards won and the number of years they received any votes: Steve Carlton (4,6); Tom Seaver (3,10); Jim Palmer (3,8); Bob Gibson (2,4); and Roger Clemens (3,6). Note that Clemens has received votes in an incredible six of his first seven years.

4 Stars. Walter "Big Train" Johnson is far and away the all-time favorite choice at pitcher. Since I need four starters on the team, I'll look to see who else is consistently in the top four. For the first fifty years of baseball, Mathewson, Young, Alexander and Grove were all consistently selected. However, modern polls have stayed only with Christy Mathewson and Lefty Grove, and have included Sandy Koufax. Bob Feller is close, but doesn't get enough mentions for a fourth star. The order of four-star winners is Johnson, Mathewson, Koufax and Grove. I listed Koufax first because Grove was not a top-three choice in the first fifty years, and while he was given the nod in the Centennial poll, Koufax got it in the *Players' Choice* and edged Grove in MVP voting.

3 Stars. Roger Clemens has not been around long enough for most polls, but his dominance of Cy Young Award attention for the past ten years heralds a very popular pitcher, and so I must insert him here. Pete Alexander, Cy Young, Bob Feller, Carl Hubbell and Warren Spahn have shown up in top-four picks numerous times, I would say in that order. Steve Carlton's best ever Cy Young Award tallies merits a third star.

2 Stars. Others who appeared in top pitcher lists in some picks are, in order, Hal Newhouser, Bob Gibson, Tom Seaver and Whitey Ford.

1 Star. Honorable mention level picks went to Rube Waddell, Lefty Gomez, Dizzy Dean, Jim Palmer, Ed Walsh and Dennis Eckersley.

PART TWO

The Selection of the All-Time Dream Team for Each Position

Chapter Five

Dream Team Outfield

Outfielders are measured by their bats. The top twenty-five hitters of all time include thirteen outfielders: Ruth, Mantle, Mays, Williams, Henderson, DiMaggio, Cobb, Robinson, Aaron, Ott, Joe Jackson, Strawberry and Speaker. The "opinion" surveys add Clemente to the list. What a list! We have three dream team positions available for them, three more on the second team, and perhaps an honorable mention or two. Each team will have a designated hitter. The task is not easy, but it's great fun. The second twenty-five hitters are obviously out of contention, given the importance of hitting, and do not have any serious contenders. The best hitter in the second twenty-five is Duke Snider, and no one has ever listed him with the best ever. So we'll focus on the thirteen mentioned above.

I removed Shoeless Joe Jackson from the start. We don't want a player we can't trust. This is not necessarily a moral position, although I'd boot him on those grounds as well. We just can't trust a guy who would take money in a big game to take a dive. I know there is a position that Joe took the money and still played to win, but it's not good enough. I don't mind what a guy does off the field, but Joe robbed baseball itself. Besides he never played in his aging years, and his numbers, probably not quite good enough anyway, would have gotten worse.

Chapter two contains the offensive stats, chapter three the available defensive information, and chapter four the opinion results. In this chapter I'll present my ranking for offense, defense and opinion recognition for each player.

The offensive ranking was heavily influenced by the

Earned Bases Average (EBA) numbers, although, as indicated, I found the need to elevate Cobb to "four-star" status. This was done in the context of my star system, which provides a principled way to adjust the EBA ranking on the basis of other career stats.

Defensive rank is similarly informed by the stats. As set forth in chapter three, we selected the stats which best measured outfield play and compared them against the league average during the player's career. This approach gave a clear picture of relative defensive accomplishment. We also evaluated other stats and considered Gold Gloves. Finally, I use the star system, which is quite helpful in making the final selection. I should remind the reader that the defensive analysis focuses only on the great hitters, and on those who appeared in the various opinion polls as all-time greats. This process added Clemente to the list. However, I had to draw the line, and the process left out several outfielders, including Max Carey, Richie Ashburn, Paul Blair, Carl Yastrzemski, Terry Moore, Al Kaline and others whose defensive prowess was not combined with enough offensive punch to rate them among the best outfielders of all-time. None of these players are seriously considered for all-time honors on anyone's list. However, their greatness is just a further testimony to the amount of talent found at the top.

The issue of how much weight to give to batting as opposed to defensive ability was discussed in chapter one. The sabermetric formulas would say that the best batters generated about seven times as many runs as the best fielders saved. I don't have a clue if that is true, and neither do the sabermetricians. But, as I said out front, hitting dominated my selection of outfielders, and defense was considered in close cases. I would note strongly that whatever dominance batting has over fielding today, it was much less so seventy-five years ago. This is why guys like Tris Speaker and Eddie Collins were favored in old-time polls over players like Ted Williams and Rogers Hornsby. Well, this dream team is a team for all time, transcending any one era of play, so I'll evaluate players in the context of their time, and give at least some deference to the perceptions about the importance of defensive play.

Here we go. The final ranking!

Final Outfielder Ranking

STAR RATING	OFFENSIVE RANKING	DEFENSIVE RANKING	A CONSENSUS OF THE OPINIONS
****	1. RUTH	1. MAYS	1. RUTH
	2. MANTLE	2. SPEAKER	2. COBB
	3. WILLIAMS		
	4. MAYS		
	5. COBB		
***	6. DIMAGGIO	3. DIMAGGIO	3. MAYS
	7. HENDERSON	4. CLEMENTE	4. DIMAGGIO
	8. ROBINSON		5. WILLIAMS
	9. AARON		
	10. OTT		
	11. STRAWBERRY		
	12. SPEAKER		
**	13. CLEMENTE	5. MANTLE	6. SPEAKER
		6. AARON	7. MANTLE
		7. HENDERSON	8. AARON
		8. ROBINSON	9. ROBINSON
		9. OTT	10. CLEMENTE
			11. OTT
*		10. COBB	12. HENDERSON
		11. RUTH	13. STRAWBERRY
0		12. WILLIAMS	
		13. STRAWBERRY	

THE FIRST TEAM

My rule is clear, in the outfield I'm looking for hitters first, far more than fielders. The heavily weighted offensive ranking alone would presumptively give the three outfield and one DH slots to Ruth, Mantle, Williams and Mays, in that order. If I were to count just stars the leaders are Mays (11); Ruth, DiMaggio, Cobb and Speaker (9); Mantle (8); Williams, Robinson, Aaron and Ott (7). However, I will evaluate all of the top players in light of all three aspects: hitting, fielding and opinion.

Following my rule, I presumptively start with the best hitters. Babe Ruth is number one there, and his offensive lead is so great that I need go no further.

First Pick, Right Field. Babe Ruth is the best baseball player who ever lived. Everybody knows it, so there can be no serious question about his placement on the All-Time Dream Team. He was number one in both the offense and opinion categories. He was certainly the greatest home run and power hitter of all time, notwithstanding Maris and Aaron having beaten his single-season and lifetime home run records. His .690 slugging average is nearly sixty points higher than the second-place mark. He was also a great hitter, boasting a .342 lifetime batting average. This was done in Yankee Stadium, *a pitcher's park*! He was so feared that he became the all-time leading walk getter with 2,056.

Before moving to the outfield, Babe was an all-star-class pitcher, winning over twenty games twice, sporting a 2.22 ERA, and improving all the time. He was only an average or slightly below-average outfielder, and this must give us some pause. But his defensive liabilities are more than offset by the size of his batting lead over all other players. Babe's EBA puts him an incredible 172 percent ahead of the average of his times. The next closest outfielder is Mantle with 156 percent, and it all starts to bunch up below 145 percent. Ruth's sabermetric score is 1,355; Williams is second at 1,093, more than three hundred points lower. By contrast, Willie Mays's putouts per game compared to the average of his times was only 25 percent above Ruth's. So, the sheer size of Ruth's batting lead overcomes any defensive difference. And if we believe the sabermetricians, batting is nearly ten times as important in generating runs than fielding is in saving them. I don't bet my life on their formulas (especially the defensive ones), but there is no question that we primarily look to hitting from outfielders. Nothing can take Babe off this team. No one is in his class in offensive production. His impact on the game was the greatest of all time, and his shadow will reach long into baseball's future.

The next candidates on the offense list are Mantle, Williams and Mays. The difference between them in adjusted and normalized EBA is only a few percentage points. However, Willie

Babe Ruth

Willie Mays

Mays is among the best defensive outfielders of all time. His glove is two levels above Mantle's and Williams's, and easily overcomes the presumption created by the few EBA point lead of Mantle and Williams. This is what has placed him well above Mickey and Ted on most all-time lists.

Second Pick, Center Field. Willie Mays is the best all-around outfielder who ever lived and, with Honus Wagner and perhaps Buck Ewing, the best all-around player. There was no better defensive outfielder, as his twelve Gold Gloves, his number-one rating in the players' survey, and countless fans attest. He is the all-time leader in outfield putouts and scored well on the sabermetric fielding formula. Tris Speaker was mighty close defensively, but Willie performed his magic with a far livelier ball to chase after. His miraculous catch of Vic Wertz's drive to deep center in the 1954 World Series is regarded as one of the great catches of all time, and is often written about in books on baseball's greatest games.

His 660 home runs is third on the all-time list, and he was strong in most other categories—hits, doubles, triples, steals. The 1951 Rookie of the Year played professional ball for the Negro Leagues at the age of fourteen. He missed most of 1952 and all of 1953 due to an army stint (and so a shot at Ruth's home run record). He was the most exciting ballplayer this side of 1950, and led all outfielders except Williams in all-time total MVP votes. He was idolized in New York, but it took some time for the fans at Candlestick Park to understand his value. It's time he was recognized for what he was, one of the greatest who ever played the game!

Third Pick, Left Field. Now for the really tough choice. Let's look at the offense list. We need to choose from Mickey Mantle, Ted Williams, Ty Cobb and Joe DiMaggio. I'm also considering a DH spot on the first team. Let's analyze this one closely.

Ty Cobb was everyone's choice for dream team outfield in the first half-century. Connie Mack said he'd "bracket Cobb and Ruth together as the two greatest ballplayers who ever lived." Robert Shoemaker, in his 1949 book *The Best in Baseball*, and Tom Meany in his 1950 *Baseball's Greatest Hitters*, both named Cobb the greatest player ever. Fred Lieb, a renowned sportswriter and baseball author, said in a 1950 article, "Hans

Wagner, Babe Ruth, Ty Cobb and Walter Johnson simply were so good they stood out like the evening star on a clear night. Anyone failing to place these immortals on his dream team would be an idiot or so biased that his views would have no value or significance." Cobb had the electric baserunning impact of a Rickey Henderson, and *also* had the highest lifetime batting average at .367. At a time when strikeouts exceeded walks by about 10 percent, Cobb had 3½ times more walks than strikeouts. David Shoebotham, in an article for *Insiders' Baseball*, measured lifetime batting averages against league averages, called a *relative batting average (RBA)*, and Cobb came out first again. In fact he had six of the top-ten annual RBA's of all time. His earned bases average places him as one of the top-ten hitters of all time, and the sabermetricians would urge that all those singles and doubles put him very close to the top in runs generated (although their formulas favor players with longer careers, like Cobb). He was a fierce and intimidating competitor, a fiery genius in analyzing how to get an edge. His presence in the game was transcendent.

But his contribution was all offense. He was only an average fielder, and while we can overlook that for the Babe, who was so far out in front offensively, we can't ignore it for Cobb. We shouldn't be intimidated by history to keep a guy on the team, especially one who's a pain in the butt. Cobb won the first MVP award ever given in 1911 at the age of twenty-six, in the midst of his prime. However, having won the award, he was ineligible again under the rules of the time. He did get some votes, however, coming in eighth, twentieth and fourteenth. The award was not given again until 1922, near the end of his career, so he only got that first one. Although named to the Centennial Team, he is, as I have noted, increasingly overlooked by contemporary opinion. This may be due to the mere passage of time or perhaps to his reputation for a greatly troubled nature and his legendary disregard for the well-being of his competitors. Let's face it, he was a miserable person. No one would give him a congeniality award, and he was resoundingly disliked and shunned by many players of his time, including his own teammates. Moreover, Detroit won only three pennants during his twenty-four seasons. Yet I'd surely want him with me and not against me. What should

Ted Williams cracks a hit.

Joe DiMaggio gets his cuts in.

we do with him? Well he has three other problems: Williams, Mantle and DiMaggio.

Ted Williams was often regarded as the best pure hitter ever. His numbers place him among the top few batters ever, certainly a player who transcended the game. He batted .344 lifetime, smacked 521 homers, drew 2,019 walks, and still served nearly five years of his prime in World War II and Korea. No outfielder garnered more MVP votes over the years. His .406 season in 1946, the last .400 season ever, is legendary, especially since he refused to sit out the last game of the season, a doubleheader, and protect the .403 average he already had. He got six hits anyway! His bat propelled him to two MVPs and two Triple Crowns. Unfortunately, it is not widely understood that Ted played in and heavily benefitted from the best hitter's park in the major leagues. As noted in chapter two, removal of the park effect puts Ted's accomplishments behind those of Ruth, Gehrig and Mantle and more in line with the other great hitters. It can also be noted that much of his batting feat occurred during and shortly after war times, when pitching and fielding were not as sharp. Furthermore, we know that Ted was a slightly below-average outfielder and base runner. A bat like his deserves to be on the first team; however, I can't have another mediocre fielder, since I already have Ruth out there. I have to rule Ted out for a field position, maybe a DH. We'll get to that later.

Let's look at "Joltin' Joe" DiMaggio. The BBWAA Centennial committee voted him the best living ballplayer a number of years back, and he is generally viewed as one of the best ever. However, his numbers raise some questions. Sure, he was exceptional, but there are some problems with a first-team pick. I was at first surprised that the fifty-year team selection committee, the All-America Board, as well as Connie Mack himself, shunned DiMaggio and Williams in favor of Tris Speaker. And they did so with conviction, since the vote tally was 12 to 1 for Speaker. DiMaggio had just finished his career, so it wasn't that they hadn't seen all of him (Ted still had ten good years left). Both Babe Ruth and Ty Cobb chose Speaker over DiMaggio and Williams in their autobiographies. It seems that Speaker's great defensive play and base-running were perceived to be more valuable than the bats of the sluggers. At best, DiMaggio can be accorded a tie with Speaker from the results of Christy Walsh's 1950 survey of five hundred sportswriters.

Yet "Joltin' Joe" DiMaggio is an all-American hero. He has transcended the game to become a part of American folklore. There is only a fraction which separates him from Mays and Speaker as the best defensive center fielder, and another hair between his overall offensive numbers and the top hitters. His all-around great play earned him three MVP awards, and his fifty-six-game hitting streak electrified America—the record most often cited as the one not likely ever to be broken. Had he played in a better hitter's park, his .325 batting average probably would have exceeded .340. Connie Mack and his All-America Board members wanted him on their all-time team, even if only as a utility outfielder, and so would I.

However, DiMaggio's failure to make Hall of Fame until after three ballots may have sent a subtle message (all other dream teamers made it on the first ballot, except Speaker who made it on the second). I'm told it was because they thought Joe would come back to play again. They didn't have to wait the five years for Hall eligibility back then. Joe had one "bad" season, a .256 year in 1951, and quit. He played only thirteen seasons, and his stock would surely have gone down if he had hung around as long as did the other greats. Anyway, my final ratings don't have Joe in the top three in offense (he did even worse on the sabermetric calculation), and his third-place defense finish doesn't elevate him enough. His three stars in batting and defense, and his curious win with the Centennial Committee herald a truly great all-around player, but they don't put him on the first team.

So, we come finally to Mickey Mantle. He is a strong number two on the batting list, with an EBA which adjusts out to being 153 percent higher than the average of his times. His home runs, 536 of them, were regularly among the longest ever hit, towering, thundering drives. He hit a 565-foot shot in Washington, and smacked one at Yankee Stadium that hit the upper-deck facade while rising. Some have estimated the shot would have traveled about six hundred feet. And he could hit them from either side of the plate, by far the best switch-hitter who ever lived. While his knees held up, he was

Ty Cobb

Mickey Mantle

a master at dragging bunts down the first base line, just past the pitcher. Mickey's great speed would then take him past the ball, the pitcher and the first baseman to the bag. Mickey's 1956 season may be the best single season ever played by anyone: He batted .353 with 52 homers and 130 RBIs. The Yankees won an amazing twelve pennants during his eighteen-year career. Had Mantle played in even an average hitter's park, his batting average would have approached .320, and had he not played during the sixties, when the strike zone was expanded, he would have done even better (same for Willie Mays). Of the top fifty hitters of all time, seventeen had over one thousand strikeouts, and twelve of these seventeen played during the sixties.

Defensively, The Mick had lightning speed and was well above average, until a spike caught in an outfield drain one day (on a fly ball hit by Willie Mays) and he twisted his knee, an injury which plagued him for the rest of his career. His legendary carousing with Billy Martin also likely cost him a step at some point. However, my rules call for a heavy emphasis and weight on batting, and Mickey's high ranking there carries a presumption of first team with it.

My dilemma here is that I respect the ability of opinion polls to preserve over time certain realities which escape the bare numbers. I refer to the intangibles which were well understood by experts and fans of the times, but which don't appear in an EBA. My rules are to look carefully at these opinions in close cases. The truth is that Mickey Mantle was generally *not* selected among the best ever, and was never said to be the best ever. Ty Cobb was routinely claimed for over sixty years to be equal to Ruth, and sometimes beyond, as the best player who ever lived. Mickey never reached these plateaus of perception. The numbers alone surely favor Mickey over Cobb and DiMaggio for the third slot on the team, but the opinions, while fading a bit, clearly favor Cobb. However, Bill James accurately points out that the best opinion is that rendered at the time a guy played. Mickey won the MVP three times and was in the top five a record nine times (so were Mays, Williams and Musial). The point is that Mickey played during an era of depressed offense and did so in a

WEIGHTED EBA		WEIGHTED LEAGUE EBA	PERCENT AHEAD OF LEAGUE
MANTLE	.535	.379	141%
COBB	.521	.378	138%
DIMAGGIO	.528	.418	126%

pitcher's park on top of it. The perceptions don't account for this, the adjusted numbers do!

I thus submit this debate as the key one in all of baseball's history. Who should get the third outfield position: Cobb, Di-Maggio or Mantle? I find it incredibly close. I have less trouble with DiMaggio, whose offensive contribution was not enough for long enough. He just doesn't have enough to overcome Mantle's numbers. But I literally shudder at the thought of taking Cobb off the first team. I can hear Fred Lieb screaming at me from the grave, "You idiot!" I searched for ways to keep Cobb on. I noted that Mantle played for eighteen years while Cobb went on for twenty-four. So I calculated where Cobb's numbers would rank if he had quit after eighteen, and it improved his adjusted EBA from .606 to .626. The league EBA during his career drops also since we cut out the lively ball part of Cobb's career from 1923 to 1928. So his new "percent ahead of his times" rises from 142 percent to 151 percent, *but he is still behind Mantle's 153 percent. And Mantle is still a better fielder.*

I still had cold feet. I knew that I was dethroning a god, and I was very unsettled about it. When I told my dad and friends I had rated Mantle over Cobb and DiMaggio they had that blank look on their faces, as if I were losing my mind. I thought about the sabermetricians, and how they would scream, "McCarthy wasn't using the correct weights for total bases in his EBA formula." Mickey's homers are only 3.15 times better than Cobb's singles. I've explained why I don't use their complex weighted stuff, but I decided to see what effect it would have here. So I reestimated my EBA formula for Mantle, Cobb and DiMaggio using the weights (3.15 homers, 2.2 triples, 1.7 doubles, 1.0 singles, .75 walks, and .42 steals). I also recalculated the EBA of the rest of the league during each player's respective career. What I found is shown in the above chart.

Now, Mantle and Joe D. had similar park effects, while

Cobb was helped by his park. So Mantle still wins out clearly. Curiously, the weights don't change things much; weighted EBA is about a one hundred points lower than the regular EBA. So much for complexity.

This is a time to stick by my rules. Many of the perceptions about Mantle do not take into account the big strike zone of the sixties, or the pitcher's park he played in. This is why we need to hang in there with the objective statistics. We need offense, and Mickey Mantle has the EBA presumption. Who can take it away from him? Also, Williams and Cobb are below him in *both* offensive and defensive ranking. Joe DiMaggio has better defensive numbers, but not by much at all. Mickey's fielding percentage is further ahead of his time's average than Joe's, and the two are nearly even on the all-important putouts per game (again, as compared to their times—see chapter three). It's only Mickey's average arm that loses out to Joe's slightly above-average arm.

Yet, Joe's slight defensive edge does not overcome Mickey's more impressive, and much more important, offensive lead. Let's be objective and let the cards fall where they may. It's time to stop the unquestioning honor and hype over Cobb and DiMaggio. Move over guys, and give it up for The Mick! His great ability to get putouts will fit nicely in left field where his average arm won't hurt us.

Ted Williams, in this case, has the numbers to clearly win the DH slot. It was not in force at the time he played, but it is for this team, and we won't need to worry about his poor fielding in this role.

So there you have it: Ruth, Mays, Mantle and Williams (DH). The best ever! Just putting these guys in the same sentence does my heart joy. Could you imagine them on the same field?

THE SECOND TEAM

First Pick, Left Field. Talk about splitting hairs! Joe DiMaggio on the second team? Well, I had to draw the line somewhere. The Yankees won an astounding ten pennants during Joe's thirteen years of play. Casey Stengel said Joe was the finest player he ever coached, but that his feats and value would not be found in the record books. This is the testimony to an all-around player who excelled in all phases of play, but wasn't number one in any of them. Every year the publicity department of the Yankees sent out a questionnaire asking who do you admire most, ninety percent of responses were for Joe. Dan Daniel wrote of Joe, "More intriguing than anything in record books was the sight of Joe in action. His stance at the plate, his bat poised, his feet only some thirty inches apart, his lethal swing truly the poetry of motion. No movement lost, no nervous jiggling of the bat, just a real pro in action. . . . Fleet without the impression of effort. Accurate, uncannily so, with the sense of direction and of diagnosis that marks the baseball genius." Joe was shy, uncomfortable in social gatherings, even moody, but on the field he was grace, power and pride, and truly one of the greatest of all time. But I've got to start Joe in left field to make room for an even greater glove.

Second Pick, Center Field. Tris Speaker was considered by everyone to be the best defensive center fielder for the first fifty years of baseball. There are a few other players ahead of him in the offensive ranking (Henderson, Robinson, Aaron, Ott, Strawberry), but their lead is only a few percentage points, and "Spoke's" defensive lead is many times greater. In the dead ball era, he played up close to second base like a fifth infielder and stole away many bloop hits, even involving himself in 139 double plays (which is what gives him such a high score on the sabermetric fielding formula, a feat impossible with the more lively ball). Speaker could also turn and run down flies overhead better than anyone in his time. Ed Bang wrote of him, "Joe Jackson one game hit a screaming line drive toward right center. It was the kind of drive that only Shoeless Joe could hit, and looked like a sure triple which would send in two runs and erase Cleveland's one run lead. Off with the crack of the bat, Speaker streaked towards the exit gate in right center. He timed his tremendous leap perfectly, and with his back to the playing field, made the catch just as he crashed into the hard wall. The momentum of the ball accentuated the thud with which he hit the concrete. He toppled head over heels and lay prostrate for several minutes, but held tight to the ball. . . . The team had suffered the tragic death of Ray Chapman and needed a lift in morale. Speaker provided the needed moment of greatness." He was voted by the nation's sportswriters in 1950 to a tie with Joe DiMaggio, and was selected above Joe D. to the dream team by the All-America Board. (I believe that players are rarely appreciated enough in their own time, because Joe D. was a better all-around player.) Tris was not much of a slugger in the dead ball days (few were!), so his EBA is not top twenty. But he was still an offensive force, batting .345 lifetime, hitting 792 doubles, 3,514 hits, and stealing 433 bases. Tris slid back a piece in the face of the great players of the last fifty years, but he is still in the hunt as an All-Time Dream Team second-teamer.

Third Pick, Right Field. This leaves Ty Cobb, Frank Robinson, Rickey Henderson, Roberto Clemente, Stan Musial, Mel Ott, Darryl Strawberry and Hank Aaron. Cobb is easy. He gets DH, end of discussion! His fielding couldn't compete with the other winners, but his offensive force was incredible, and he was clearly the best player of all time on the base paths.

Henderson is still playing, and while his all-time records for baserunning catapulted him into contention (along with a substantial "park effect" adjustment), few fans would seriously consider him for dream-team honors over the field I have listed. His offensive and defensive numbers alone, however, make him a very close choice for second team, and again it seems we are dealing with slight differences. His EBA and batting runs rankings are sixth and eleventh respectively, and defense is ranked seventh among the nominees. However, he has only one MVP, and has really not received that many MVP votes over the years, under one thousand in his first dozen years. His often surly and selfish attitude has followed him around the league in several trades and certainly has detracted from his game. Hustle and a great love for the game are ingredients for the all-time team. Rickey seems to fall short in these categories. Strawberry and Ott are also out. Their bats were great, but not good enough to get them into the top nine. Their fielding was not exceptional (though Ott had a great arm) and thus does not help their case at all. Few, if any, modern-day fans would suggest Strawberry for such honor; certainly the Mets didn't think highly enough of him to keep him. And Mel Ott was not picked by the nation's sportswriters and Connie Mack on their first fifty years of baseball dream team. He was behind Ruth, Cobb, Speaker and DiMaggio then, and the presence of Aaron in the second fifty years does not advance Henderson's ranking.

So, I've got one slot left for either Hank Aaron or Frank Robinson. The choice should be relatively simple since their careers covered essentially the same years. But only a percentage point separates their "percent ahead of their times" rating. Henry Aaron was truly a great player, and his all-time home run record will last at least until the next century. His defense is short of Mays's and Speaker's, but three Gold Gloves and a decent sabermetric score place him in clear contention for the second team. Moreover, Hank was rated sixth in the players' survey, and consistently scored high in MVP voting. His last five years produced the needed 116 homers to catch Ruth, but also led to generally below-average hitting for him.

Frank Robinson also was a superstar. This Rookie of the Year winner smacked 586 homers en route to two MVPs and a Triple Crown. However, while Frank and Hank were close offensively, Hank had the clearly better glove and a far superior arm. Robinson won no Gold Gloves. Hank also outpolled Frank in MVP votes by a career score of 1,722 to 1,239. The players' survey gives the nod to Hank, and so do I.

I haven't talked much about Stan Musial yet. He played his career half in the outfield and half at first base. I remember him mainly as a first baseman. His offense and defense outfield stats did not qualify for a first team slot, and his best shot is at first base. I have him and the likes of Jimmie Foxx fighting it out in the next chapter, at least for a second team first base role. Tune in then.

There you have the second team outfield: DiMaggio, Speaker and Aaron; Ty Cobb is the designated hitter.

I'm giving honorable mentions to Rickey Henderson for his all-time stolen base record, to Pete Rose for his most hits ever, to Frank Robinson for his Triple Crown and consistent exceptional play, and to Roberto Clemente for the best arm ever.

Chapter Six

Dream Team First Base

The top ten hitters of all time, and forty-three of the top fifty, were either outfielders or first basemen! So it's pretty clear where the sluggers play defense. First base is even more of a hitting position. It is used more for those players who perhaps can't field quite as well as others, or who are slower or maybe have lost a step with age.

The nominees for dream team first basemen are: Lou Gehrig, Jimmie Foxx, Dick Allen, Johnny Mize, Hank Greenberg, Dan Brouthers, Stan Musial, Willie McCovey, George Sisler, Bill Terry and Hal Chase. The first eight are nominated because they are among the top twenty-five hitters of all time. This "cut off" excludes guys like Willie Stargell, Harmon Killebrew and Norm Cash, but I had to cut it somewhere. Sisler, Terry and Chase are among the nominees because they were either listed as number one in past surveys (Sisler), or named by others knowledgeable about the game (Terry, Chase). However, Hal Chase is on and right off again, since he was bounced from the game for taking dives. As with Joe Jackson, we can't have someone we can't trust! He wouldn't make this team anyway.

My approach will be to rank each player in the three categories: offense, defense and opinion ratings, similar to the way we analyzed outfielders.

For offense I start with the "percent ahead of their time" adjusted EBA ranking from chapter two. This creates a presumptive ranking. In the defense category, there is a real problem due to the screwed-up way the stats are counted. "Putouts" include *all* outs at first base. This means that snaring a hot grounder unassisted or going back for a foul pop-up counts the same as catching a force-out throw from another infielder. They are all lumped together. It makes the putout stat useless. In chapter three I relied upon assists per game as compared to league averages. I also considered the number of times a player led the league in certain statistical categories, particularly the number of Gold Gloves they were awarded.

Finally, the opinion category presents the opinions and perceptions which surveyed over time. I draw heavily from the 1950 All-America Board survey, the Centennial Team picks, the *Players' Choice* survey, MVP voting, and selected other opinions.

For each category, I employ the star system, which groups and rates players by general level of performance.

As noted, many more players seem to have played first base as a second position than any other spot on the diamond. It is particularly well-suited for older players near the ends of their careers, men who have more punch in their bats than in their legs. Of course, this is less true today since the DH rule in the American league allows older players to not play defense at all. My ratings attempt to analyze players at the position they played for most of their career. Stan Musial is one difficult exception, since he played a great deal at two positions during his career. He actually played a few more games in the outfield, but fans and players seem to remember him more at first base. I have included him with first basemen, but it did not affect his outcome one way or the other since his value was in his bat and not his glove. Pete Rose is another who played everywhere, and again it did not affect him since his numbers, affirmed by opinion polls, do not place him high enough for serious consideration. "Charlie Hustle" was a good hitter — a very good hitter — who played long enough to accumulate the most hits ever. But he is just among the all-time *great* hitters.

A few words about the ranking which appears on page 96. The hitting ranks are taken directly from the stats in chapter two. The fielding ranks are taken directly from chapter three's analysis, and the opinion rankings flow from chapter four.

Final First Base Ranking

STAR RATING	OFFENSIVE RANKING	DEFENSIVE RANKING	A CONSENSUS OF THE OPINIONS
****	1. GEHRIG	1. TERRY	1. GEHRIG
	2. FOXX		
***	3. MUSIAL	2. SISLER	2. SISLER
	4. ALLEN		3. MUSIAL
	5. MIZE		4. FOXX
	6. GREENBERG		
	7. MCCOVEY		
	8. BROUTHERS		
**	9. TERRY	3. FOXX	5. TERRY
	10. SISLER	4. MUSIAL	6. GREENBERG
		5. GREENBERG	
		6. MIZE	
*		7. GEHRIG	7. MIZE
		8. BROUTHERS	8. BROUTHERS
			9. ALLEN
			10. MCCOVEY
0		9. ALLEN	
		10. MCCOVEY	

FIRST TEAM

Lou Gehrig, end of story. The All-America Board had rocks in their heads to pick Sisler. Gehrig just leaps out at you from the above chart. Terry and Sisler were great fielders, but this is a slugger's position, and we need offense at first base! Gehrig was much further in front of Sisler in offense, than was Sisler in front of Gehrig in defense.

Lou was by far the best hitting first baseman ever. He ranks first in our offensive EBA rankings, and also in the sabermetric measure. His adjusted EBA was .723, second only to Ruth. His lifetime batting average was .340. He hit screaming doubles, triples and homers, and struck out only half as often as

Jimmie Foxx

Lou Gehrig

most sluggers on his way to two MVPs and a Triple Crown. He was known as the "Iron Horse" as much for his steely muscular build as for his all-time, and perhaps unbeatable (watch out for Ripken!), record for playing in 2,130 straight games. This is a legacy that will rarely be undertaken in this age of pampered millionaires. David Falkner reported in *Nine Sides of the Diamond* that Lou was x-rayed once and found to have had seventeen fractures in his hand. Yet he never missed a game.

Gehrig was not a great fielder, but became a decent one. Harry Grayson said of Lou in his book, *They Played the Game*, that "He was a poor fielder at first, but never stopped trying until he overcame all his faults." Our rules don't worry too much about defense at first base. A great defender adds only marginally to winning there. We need hitting, and Lou is clearly the best at that. He was the clear winner in nearly all opinion polls, and is with me also.

SECOND TEAM

The top rankings for the three categories in the table on page 96 include two other players who appear in at least one of the 4-Star columns: Jimmie Foxx and Bill Terry. George Sisler had a great glove, and Stan Musial is third in batting. George and Stan both rate high in the opinion category. We'll look at all four for second team honors. Dick Allen was fourth in batting but was generally regarded as an under-performer, and can't compete with the four I listed. Besides he is not in the Hall of Fame, so that excludes him anyway. Mize, Greenberg and Brouthers were exceptional hitters, but have no other credits to elevate them here above the other four candidates.

Of George Sisler, Connie Mack said this: "Sisler was as graceful and capable as anyone I ever saw. He was a great hitter too, and had exceptional team spirit. Like Ruth he was a very good left-handed pitcher." Mack ultimately voted for Gehrig as first baseman on the All-America team, although the full thirteen-member selection committee gave first-team honor to Sisler. Sisler had a very good bat, a .340 lifetime batting average. But, his .468 slugging average doesn't compete with Foxx's .600. He was not among the top fifty batters

Stan Musial

measured by EBA, and was not even in the top one hundred in Thorn and Palmer's batting runs measure. Sisler's offensive production was not enough, even against a standard which considers his defensive ability during the "bunt and run" theatrics of the dead ball era.

Bill Terry was also absent from my Top Fifty Hitters list, but just barely since his "percent ahead of his times" stat was about 126 percent, ten points over Sisler. He was found at seventieth in Thorn and Palmer's all-time batting rating. The

Players' Choice survey rated Sisler sixth overall (and only fifth all time for defense), while Terry was rated seventh. I simply can't overcome the strong presumption in favor of offense under my rules for first base and put either Sisler or Terry on the dream team. Particularly Terry, who played with a lively ball, and so is even more subject than Sisler to the "dominance of offense" rule for first basemen. We require slugging, driving offense from first basemen.

Having eliminated the others, we come back to Foxx and Musial. Both players won three MVPs; Foxx also smashed his way to a coveted Triple Crown. Foxx was rated only fifth by the five hundred sportswriters who voted in the All-America Board poll for the first fifty-year team. That committee ranked Sisler, Terry and Chase ahead of him, and we've already dealt with them. The board's eye for defense, especially in picking Sisler over Gehrig, showed a love for good-looking baseball, too much at the expense of winning. As stated earlier, I share some of those views, but I'm not crazy! Jimmie Foxx was a major force in baseball, and a super glove, too. Why he is overlooked in polls, such as the Centennial pick, amazes me. Perhaps it was his drinking, and the vote became more of a morals issue.

Musial got more of the more recent *Players' Choice* votes and was consistently higher in MVP voting than Foxx during their respective careers. Stan got one thousand more hits and three hundred more doubles than Jimmie, and only fifty fewer homers, *but he also batted nearly three thousand more times*. It's close, but it seems that "Stan the Man" comes up short of overtaking the presumption of Foxx's higher rankings. Jimmie Foxx outranked all others offensively. He was better than Musial defensively, certainly no worse. Musial doesn't have enough to overcome the presumption of Foxx's higher EBA rank. Jimmie Foxx gets second team! Stan Musial gets honorable mention.

Chapter Seven

Dream Team Second Base

y Top Fifty Hitters of All Time include five second basemen. They are Rogers Hornsby, Joe Morgan, Ross Barnes, Eddie Collins and Nap Lajoie. The opinion polls add Charlie Gehringer and Frankie Frisch to the list. Bill Mazerowski usually comes up on top when considering only defense, but his merely average bat (EBA .402, BA .260) has kept him out of the top three on anyone's list of the greatest second basemen ever. He is also not in the Hall of Fame, having been passed up many times, so he will not be included here.

A couple of modern-day players, Bobby Grich and Ryne Sandberg, are not yet eligible for the Hall, but will be looked at here.

Ross Barnes, though, is off. This clever second baseman from the earliest days of baseball tallied only seven years in the official statistics, beginning in 1871. We have only 1,032 at bats to work with, and that's far too few for consideration. He's also not in the Hall of Fame, and my rules exclude him on that count also.

I looked at the offensive and defensive stats of the other Hall of Fame second basemen. Bobby Doerr, Johnny Evers, Billy Herman and Red Schoendienst had impressive numbers, but were just not up to the others. Doerr had the best shot since he was one of the best ever at the double play, but his EBA of .514 was aided by Fenway Park, and was only a hair over average for his time after adjustments. Without opinion votes or an MVP to help, he could not make the short list. Rod Carew made the Hall of Fame in 1992 and got one MVP for his great slapsticking, but he was clearly average defensively. That, plus just a .502 EBA, makes him an automatic out at second base.

Jackie Robinson came to us in his twenty-eighth year, and we missed much of his greatness. He played only four years steadily at second base, and we just did not see enough of him to move the others aside. The ban on blacks in the major leagues is the worst blight in all of baseball's history, and a matter of deep anguish for me in writing this book. A few times I considered chucking the whole thing when wondering how fair it was to pass over such great players as Robinson and Satchel Paige because their numbers were robbed by racism. I continued, however, because of our shared love for the game, and because a silent protest is not heard. But I continue with the knowledge that no one will ever be able to come up with the true All-Time Dream Team due to the color ban.

The top eight candidates for the second base short list are clearly the right choices, and, with the exception of Robinson, no one has claimed anyone else for all-time best honors.

When we did the selection for outfield and first base, we weighed hitting as much more important than defense. Hitting is key to every field position, yet we see a most interesting development as we move into the infield, especially up the middle. The opinion polls don't just pay homage to the best hitters. The balance shifts to weigh defense more heavily. The reason is well understood by players and knowledgeable fans, and it is objectively approximated by Thorn and Palmer's *fielding runs* statistic. The number of runs saved by the great middle infielders is nearly *double* that saved by the great outfielders (232 average runs saved by the top ten second basemen as compared to 135 by the top ten outfielders). Viewing the competition against sabermetric statistics makes for interesting comparisons. While Rogers Hornsby's 859 "batting runs generated" was nearly 300 runs higher than Nap Lajoie's total, Nap's 370 "fielding runs saved" was 459 runs higher than Hornsby's -89. The sabermetricians would argue that Lajoie's fielding saved nearly 160 more runs than Hornsby generated.

Yet even among second basemen, the average estimate of runs generated by the top five hitting second basemen was still nearly double the runs saved by the top five fielding sec-

Jackie Robinson

ond basemen. So we face a situation where the stats suggest that, while defense up the middle infield is much more important than in the outfield, offense is still a more important overall consideration.

Still, we see that the opinion polls tend to weigh infield defense a bit more highly than batting. So, there is a substantial difference of opinion in how much to weigh offense versus defense. Now, I'm not going along too far with these sabermetric defensive formulas, for reasons I stated earlier. Simply put, I don't trust a defensive statistic that doesn't have Willie Mays among the top ten outfielders, Gil Hodges among the top ten first basemen, or Charlie Gehringer among the top ten second basemen, and that says Brooks Robinson was only the fifth-best defensive third baseman. But the sabermetric defensive formulas at least provide us with some insight on balancing batting and fielding for middle infielders.

My rule in selecting the dream team second baseman will be to insist on greatness in fielding first, and then look for batting ability. Weakness in either category will be fatal, which is why guys like Doerr, Carew, Evers, Herman and Schoendienst, and also Mazerowski, are not considered. My rule represents a bit of a compromise between the favoritism for defense which we see in polls which often pick a George Sisler or a Brooks Robinson over far superior hitters, and the reality that batting is what ultimately wins games. Beautiful baseball deserves a place along with winning baseball. My rule eliminates average fielders, no matter how well they can hit!

BATTING

Again, the batting stats are straight out of the calculator. Since only three of the above second basemen made the Top Fifty Hitters list in chapter two, I'll include some of the numbers here for reference.

The EBAs for this batting table were adjusted to reflect the park effect, as described in chapter two. EBA/A/N reflects that this stat is further normalized to league average, and as such it gives the "percent ahead of his time" for hitting. BR/A, the sabermetric formula for estimated runs generated, is adjusted and normalized also. Hornsby is clearly out in front of the pack, the difference between the rest is quite small.

PLAYER	YEARS	AB	H	2B	3B	HR	SB	PARK EFF.	BA	BR/A	EBA/A/N
HORNSBY	1915-37	8,173	2,930	541	169	301	135	101.6%	.358	859	.627/142%
MORGAN	1963-84	9,277	2,517	449	96	268	722	90.6%	.271	470	.584/135%
E. COLLINS	1906-30	9,949	3,311	437	187	47	744	100.0%	.333	613	.553/128%
LAJOIE	1896-16	9,589	3,242	657	163	83	380	96.0%	.338	567	.538/127%
GEHRINGER	1924-42	8,860	2,839	574	146	184	181	104.2%	.320	339	.552/119%
SANDBERG	1981-93	7,161	2,080	340	67	240	323	106.0%	.290	174	.518/116%
GRICH	1970-86	6,890	1,833	320	47	224	104	92.4%	.266	259	.522/116%
FRISCH	1919-37	9,112	2,880	466	138	105	419	104.2%	.316	144	.500/112%

DEFENSE

Let's take a quick look at the key stats from chapter three. Unlike those for outfield and first base, here the defensive ranking creates a presumption for selection to the All-Time Dream Team, which then must be clearly overcome by other categories. Keep in mind that the "league averages" considers regular players only so the percent above the actual average is higher.

The defensive ranking is taken directly from chapter three, where we compared putouts per game, assists per game, double plays per game and fielding percentage against the average stats of journeymen second-sackers of each player's era. We also considered Gold Gloves and some opinion information.

I note here that while Lajoie and Collins were both given four stars, since their stats were a class ahead of the rest, Lajoie was 58 percent ahead of his time in double plays per game, while Collins was only 16 percent ahead. Thus, Lajoie's defensive lead is significant.

Furthermore, the defensive difference between Lajoie and Hornsby is enormous, many times greater than Hornsby's batting lead.

OPINIONS

The opinion results are pretty straightforward, and are analyzed in chapter four. Although neither of them has a clear consensus, Gehringer and Hornsby polled one and two re-

Napoleon Lajoie

Rogers Hornsby

Percentage Comparison of Fielding Stats of Final Second Base Candidates Compared to the Average Player of the Time

PLAYER	FA MINUS LEAGUE AVER.	PO/G DIVIDED BY LEAGUE AVER.	A/G DIVIDED BY LEAGUE AVER.	DP/G DIVIDED BY LEAGUE AVER.
LAJOIE	+.014	+18%	+7%	+58%
E. COLLINS	+.015	+17%	+2%	+16%
GRICH	+.006	+16%	+15%	+23%
SANDBERG	+.008	+2%	+20%	+00%
GEHRINGER	+.010	−1%	+7%	+11%
MORGAN	+.004	+10%	+10%	+1%
FRISCH	+.006	+3%	+6%	+7%
HORNSBY	−.003	−14%	+3%	+2%

spectively in both major surveys, the 1950 writers' survey and the later *Players' Choice* survey. Hornsby finally passed him in the Centennial vote. Eddie Collins got some smart votes and did well whenever there was an MVP vote. Joe Morgan is a contemporary favorite. The surveys seem to have forgotten about Lajoie, who started his career in 1896. He was "King Larry" during his time, and rates way above others on the sabermetric formulas. His high level of putouts, double plays and assists during the days of rutted fields is phenomenal. The great writer Fred Lieb wrote in rebuttal to Lajoie's absence on the first-fifty-years team, "I find it hard to understand why Nap Lajoie and Rogers Hornsby did not fare better in the balloting. . . . It may be that the men taking part in the nominating ballot have forgotten about Lajoie . . . he was the most graceful of players. The only players ever to compare with him in grace were Hal Chase and Charley Gehringer. Lajoie glided over the ground with the graceful ease of a panther. . . . Like the later-day Gehringer he had an uncanny knack of being in the right spot for most of the hitters." Donald Honig gave this view in *Baseball America*: "Lajoie never quite caught the public imagination as did contemporaries Mathewson or Wagner. . . . Graceful he was and hit line drives that could break an infielder's shinbones. . . . That's what we

Final Second Base Ranking

STAR RATING	OFFENSIVE RANKING	DEFENSIVE RANKING	A CONSENSUS OF OPINION
****	1. HORNSBY	1. LAJOIE	
		2. E. COLLINS	
***	2. MORGAN	3. GRICH	1. GEHRINGER
	3. E. COLLINS	4. SANDBERG	2. HORNSBY
	4. LAJOIE	5. GEHRINGER	3. E. COLLINS
			4. LAJOIE
			5. MORGAN
**	5. GEHRINGER	6. MORGAN	6. FRISCH
	6. SANDBERG	7. FRISCH	
	7. GRICH		
	8. FRISCH		
*		8. HORNSBY	7. SANDBERG
			8. GRICH

hear fifty years later. That was the arrived consensus, and today it is not enough, nor apparently was it then!" Well, maybe Honig never made it to Cleveland where they named the whole team after Nap, and crowned him "King Larry." I still think Lajoie seems more forgotten than ignored, but I reported the results as they came in.

THE FIRST TEAM

Sorry, Rajah! Hornsby doesn't make the first team, or the second team for that matter, but the greatest hitting second baseman ever, one of the best pure hitters ever, deserves some opening comments beyond the mere honorable mention I will give him. His .358 lifetime batting average is second only to Ty Cobb. His bat smashed his way to two Triple Crowns, and two MVP awards. Thorn and Palmer state hypothetically that he would have had three more MVPs if the award had started earlier in his career.

However, the glove up the middle is critical, and Rajah's

was only an average one, at best. His autobiography, *My Kind of Baseball*, talks almost exclusively of hitting. J. Roy Stockton's introduction describes the Rajah as a "steady fielder." The dream team needs more than "steady." Teammate Specs Torporcer, in an interview with Lawrence Ritter in *The Glory of Their Times*, said he once replaced Hornsby at second for a short time, moving Hornsby to the outfield. He said, "Hornsby was always weak on pop flies, which is annoying for a second baseman but catastrophic for an outfielder." We have some superb fielders who were also great hitters, and the pollsters and opinions have agreed with a defensive priority in every case. Hornsby's offensive lead is significant, but by no means substantial enough to overcome my rules requiring defense up the middle. According to my rules, Hornsby's position on the dream team would be assured if his defensive play were at least well above average, but his putouts were well below average. The 1-Star defensive rating itself was already quite generous.

Hornsby also had an attitude, and this is what led to his repeatedly being traded. Bill James said, "So what do you have? You have a great hitter and a fine base runner who is a bad defensive second baseman and a pain in the butt! Too many people had him and just couldn't wait to get rid of him. Nobody ever wanted to get rid of a Mays, Mantle or Musial. They traded Hornsby because they wanted to get rid of Rogers Hornsby." His teams won only three pennants in twenty-three years, so he hardly can be said to have been a positive force. Well, I have enough trouble already with Ty Cobb on the second team (especially when he finds out he's only pinch hitting), and I don't need any more head cases. Rogers Hornsby will get an honorable mention to keep alive the memory of his great bat and his healthy approach to the game he loved.

If Hornsby had got no great glove, then Charlie Gehringer, the opinion polls' favorite, had no great bat (only 19 percent ahead of the average player of his time)! Gehringer did not make any top-fifty list for offense. So, even though he is a favorite, the numbers just don't justify it. He didn't get four stars in any category. It took seven ballots to get Gehringer into the Hall of Fame (Morgan took one, Lajoie three, Collins four, Hornsby five and Frisch seven).

Eddie Collins

So, it's a battle between Eddie Collins, Nap Lajoie and Joe Morgan for the first team position! Our defensive ranking lists Lajoie and Collins as excellent all-time defensive second basemen, with Lajoie enjoying a noticeable edge. Everybody agrees that they were defensively the best in the game during their respective careers, and opinions vary as to who was better. My analysis confirms the sabermetric formula in this case. Nap Lajoie is clearly the better glove. He set a double-play-per-game ratio that was an incredible 58 percent ahead of his time.

Morgan and Collins were the better offensive threats, *but only slightly*. Lajoie was just one EBA point behind Collins when compared to their respective times. All three made the Top Fifty EBA list, but Lajoie was rated between Collins and Morgan on the SABR theoretical runs-generated list.

Morgan's home run power gives him a clear power edge. Collins's higher batting average and longer career gave him an edge with the sabermetric runs-generated formula. All three were terrors on the bases. Lajoie wasn't quite the speedster, but compensated by hitting so many more doubles. These guys are close indeed. Collins was a smart player and a great leader, and the intangibles, the unmeasurables, are what put him ahead in the polls.

This is certainly the closest battle of all. But, I shall not do what has apparently been done by others—that is, ignore or forget the old-timers. My rules out front were to get the best defense I could at second base. Nap Lajoie was, pretty clearly, the best. Lajoie was also a great offensive producer, with only the width of a modern-day bat stem separating the offensive ability of him and Collins! Lajoie's lead in defense was greater than Collins's razor-thin lead in offense. I give first team to Larry "Nap" Lajoie. Hail the King!

SECOND TEAM

Now it's down to Collins or Morgan. I include Morgan because, even though the difference between him and two modern-day guys, Grich and Sandberg, was slight on defense, Joe had a far superior bat. I gave Joe only two stars on defense, but he was very close to a third star.

The stat that broke the tie for me was that Collins was in the top five in MVP voting each of the seven years that it was available to him, except for one year when he was sixth. It was available from 1911 to 1914, and again from 1922 to 1924. That's enough for me. Collins was a whole class, or two, above Morgan in defense. I'm going with Eddie Collins. Ty Cobb said Hornsby couldn't catch a fly, Lajoie (while graceful) couldn't cover a lot of ground, but "Collins could do it all!" (And Cobb only saw Lajoie in the second half of his career.) Eddie Collins is my second team choice.

Joe Morgan was at the heart of the second- or third-best team ever assembled. I won't pass him up completely. His glove clearly is up with the better second basemen, and his 268 homers are in Hornsby's league. Along with Rajah and Jackie Robinson, he gets an honorable mention.

Chapter Eight

Dream Team Shortstop

I could probably just say two words—Honus Wagner—and be out of this chapter! And nobody would wrinkle their brows in the slightest. Fred Lieb said in his rebuttal to the fifty-year team, "The oddest thing to me about the shortstop poll is that any votes were cast other than those for Wagner." Well, we do have to contend with second team choices, and, let's face it, Honus Wagner deserves a lot more than two words. Also, it gets a lot closer than you think when you look at a few other guys. The Wagner bulldozer may have rolled on alone for years, but no more! Second place is drawing nearer!

Much of what I said about second basemen applies here, with perhaps a bit less emphasis on defense. I say *less*, surprisingly, since a review of the total chances per game and total putouts indicates that second basemen see a bit more defensive action than shortstops. But we clearly need to ensure defensive ability up the middle, since that's where most runs are scored or stopped (except of course for those scored in the bleachers). Also, the shortstop needs a great arm to fire the ball across the diamond.

There are sixteen shortstops in the Hall of Fame. Three of them have received MVP awards: Ernie Banks and Cal Ripken got two, and Lou Boudreau got one. Phil Rizzuto and Marty Marion each got one MVP but are not in the Hall of Fame (though both should be!). However, my rules drop both of them from the short list for that reason, and their stats don't warrant an exception. Marion was fourth in the *Players' Choice* poll and second in the fifty-year poll, and it beats me why he was placed higher than some of the others. Robin

Yount got an MVP too and, as with Ripken, is an active player as I write this. Luis Aparicio was a Rookie of the Year, and received nine Gold Gloves, second only to Ozzie Smith's eleven. The latter four active players also will make the short list of candidates here.

I looked at the other Hall of Famers. Joe Cronin and Arky Vaughan put out some good offense, while Rabbit Maranville and Dave Bancroft had some great defensive numbers. They all make the short list for further analysis, although my rule for greatness in both offense and defense up the middle will sorely challenge them. Hughie Jennings clearly showed all-around ability and makes the list easily. As for the others, there wasn't quite enough to get them on the short list. I'm not sure how Bill James got Luke Appling all the way to second place on his all-time list, since Appling's EBA was only .482 and his fielding only a hair above the average of his contemporaries.

OPINIONS

The clearest thing about the shortstop position is the opinions over time. Honus Wagner wins all polls and surveys and every individual opinion I have come across. At the 3-Star level, Ernie Banks for his power and Luis Aparicio for his glove take the next two slots. After that we drop another level and it becomes less clear with Joe Cronin and Lou Boudreau picking up some rays of the public spotlight. Cal Ripken has only twelve years in, so was not around for most polls (but watch him!). Ozzie Smith is in the same boat, although his magic glove has gathered attention and just may be the best ever.

More than with any other position, we see a flip-flop with the best gloves having the worst bats, and vice versa. Maranville, Smith and Aparicio are examples: superstar gloves but average hitters.

I will cut off all but the top seven fielders from further review because that's where the great gloves end. I agree with Bill James that Yount and Banks are underrated at defense; both got a Gold Glove. But we are looking for the very best defense here. Frankly, the very best probably end with Bancroft.

OFFENSE

Again, the batting stats are straight out of the calculator. Since only one shortstop made the Top Fifty list in chapter two (guess who!), I'll include some numbers here for reference.

PLAYER	YEARS	AB	H	2B	3B	HR	SB	PARK EFF.	BA	BR/A	EBA/A/N
WAGNER	1897-17	10,430	3,630	640	252	101	722	99.3%	.327	652	.574/135%
VAUGHAN	1932-48	6,622	2,103	356	128	96	356	102.0%	.318	356	.529/122%
BANKS	1953-71	9,421	2,583	407	90	512	50	106.0%	.274	261	.520/118%
CRONIN	1926-45	7,579	2,285	515	118	170	87	105.5%	.301	229	.522/115%
RIPKEN	1981-93	7,579	2,086	395	37	297	33	93.0%	.275	229	.524/114%
JENNINGS	1891-18	4,904	1,527	232	88	18	359	101.3%	.311	147	.510/113%
BOUDREAU	1938-52	6,029	1,779	385	68	68	51	96.2%	.295	181	.497/112%
YOUNT	1974-93	11,008	3,142	583	126	251	271	97.0%	.285	225	.496/109%
O. SMITH	1978-93	8,632	2,265	369	63	23	563	98.3%	.262	–101	.445/100%
BANCROFT	1915-30	7,182	2,004	320	77	32	145	100.9%	.279	8	.433/ 99%
MARANVILLE	1912-35	10,078	2,605	380	177	28	291	96.8%	.258	–240	.415/ 95%
APARICIO	1956-73	10,230	2,677	394	93	83	506	99.0%	.262	-246	.410/ 94%

THE FIRST TEAM

Honus Wagner. No doubt about it! Honus Wagner is often ranked with Ruth, Cobb and Mays as one of the greatest ever, certainly as an all-around player. He batted .327, was a slugger in the dead ball era, was the best base runner of his time (722 steals), and had the surest glove of any shortstop ever. The story goes that Honus went after a grounder one day when a jackrabbit darted across the field. He promptly caught the rabbit and flipped it to first, beating the runner "by a hare." He was a popular player, and a player's player.

Wagner was among the best of fielders. He was not among the top few overall, but unlike Rogers Hornsby at second, who was below average, Honus was clearly a great defensive player. Admittedly, his assists per game back in the dead ball days was only average, which indicates less-than-great range. But, his hands were magnificent — the best ever — and once he got to the ball his arm was sure.

Percentage Comparison of Fielding Stats of Final Shortstop Candidates Compared to the Average Player of the Time

At the risk of drowning you in stats, I've brought forward the key defensive analysis for ease of review. It's critical for shortstops, and it shows that the top eight or nine are all great fielders.

PLAYER	FA MINUS LEAGUE AVER.	PO/G DIVIDED BY LEAGUE AVER.	A/G DIVIDED BY LEAGUE AVER.	DP/G DIVIDED BY LEAGUE AVER.
O. SMITH	+.014	+22%	+34%	+19%
APARICIO	+.008	+33%	+14%	+22%
RIPKEN	+.013	+17%	+22%	+28%
MARANVILLE	+.011	+21%	+15%	+17%
JENNINGS	+.005	+29%	+11%	+31%
WAGNER	+.023	+14%	+1%	+17%
BANCROFT	+.003	+26%	+18%	+15%
BOUDREAU	+.015	+6%	+5%	+23%
YOUNT	+.000	+26%	+18%	+25%
BANKS	+.007	+20%	+14%	+12%
CRONIN	+.002	+1%	+8%	+8%
VAUGHAN	+.002	+1%	+8%	–3%

Now, I must reckon that the standard for up the middle is defense first, and Honus has a number of players ahead of him. The thing is that, among the better gloves, only Ripken and Jennings could hit well enough to even be considered. Jennings's defensive edge is slight, nowhere near enough to consider him seriously. But Ripken. . . . I'm tempted. He is a super fielder and a slugger who hit 297 home runs by 1993. At this time his consecutive starts total 1,897 and he has the only chance among today's players to match Gehrig's "Iron Horse" record of 2,130 straight games. However, Wagner is still far in front offensively, and the defensive lead of these other players is slight. I want great defense at short, which Wagner will give me, and he will bring an all-time great bat,

Honus Wagner

too. He has played half again as many years as Ripken at the time of this writing. But, we'll keep a real close eye on Cal.

SECOND TEAM

In the meantime, Cal will occupy the number two spot. I have him rated a bit over Jennings both in offense and in defense. Ernie Banks is a close fourth, but his EBA is only a few points ahead of Ripken's. Sure, Ernie had those 512 home runs, fantastic for a shortstop, but he only went for homers, batting .274, uncommonly striking out 1,236 times with only 763 walks, and lost three bases more than he stole! He had a decent glove, better than he was usually given credit for, but was not in Ripken's league. Let's see what the next ten years do to the Wagner mystique. Cal could catch fire, but it's not likely since 1992 and 1993 were not great years for him.

Final Shortstop Ranking

STAR RANKING	OFFENSIVE RANKING	DEFENSIVE RANKING	A CONSENSUS OF THE OPINIONS
****		1. O. SMITH	1. WAGNER
		2. APARICIO	
		3. MARANVILLE	
		4. RIPKEN	
***	1. WAGNER	5. JENNINGS	
		6. WAGNER	
		7. BANCROFT	
**	2. VAUGHAN	8. BOUDREAU	2. BANKS
	3. BANKS	9. YOUNT	3. MARION
	4. RIPKEN	10. BANKS	4. CRONIN
	5. CRONIN		5. APARICIO
	6. JENNINGS		6. BOUDREAU
	7. BOUDREAU		
	8. YOUNT		
*	9. O. SMITH	11. CRONIN	7. RIPKEN +
	10. BANCROFT	12. VAUGHAN	8. O. SMITH +
	11. MARANVILLE		9. MARANVILLE
	12. APARICIO		10. BANCROFT
			11. JENNINGS
			12. VAUGHAN

+ = Not rated

Chapter Nine

Dream Team Third Base

T he *hot corner* requires its own unique blend of offensive and defensive ability. It's one of the beauties of baseball that each position seeks its own blend of athletic traits. The total number of plays per game for the top third basemen (about four per game) falls between that of outfielders (three per game) and that of the middle infielders (about 6.5). The sabermetric formulas would suggest that batting still generates several times as many runs as fielding saves, although the opinions of players and experts again testify that defense is far more important than that. My approach will be to seek a balance, but one which ensures the best batting. Unlike my outfield criteria, well-above-average defensive ability is a must.

The players on my short list have many demands on them. There are seven third basemen in the Hall of Fame: Frank "Home Run" Baker, Jimmy Collins, George Kell, Fred Lindstrom, Eddie Mathews, Brooks Robinson and Pie Traynor. There are also a number of as yet ineligibles to also consider. Mike Schmidt is eligible in 1994 and seems sure to make it on the first ballot. Schmidt and Mathews were the only third sackers on my Top Fifty Hitters list. George Brett is still playing and, along with Schmidt and Robinson, won an MVP. Schmidt, in fact, won three of them! Wade Boggs has the highest modern-day batting average and also is still active. There are other names which come to the fore: Ron Santo, Ken Boyer, Bill Madlock, Graig Nettles. But none of them is in the Hall, which knocks them off my team. Santo deserves the Hall, certainly more than Lindstrom, and I also expect to see Nettles there someday. But these guys will never threaten the top

OFFENSE

PLAYER	YEARS	AB	H	2B	3B	HR	SB	PARK EFF.	BA	BR/<u>A</u>	EBA/<u>A</u>/N
MATHEWS	1952-68	8,537	2,315	354	72	512	68	89.8%	.271	531	.609/137%
SCHMIDT	1972-89	8,352	2,234	408	59	548	99	98.1%	.295	561	.591/134%
BAKER	1908-22	5,984	1,838	315	103	96	235	101.9%	.307	246	.511/121%
BRETT	1973-93	10,349	3,154	665	137	317	201	103.0%	.305	506	.538/118%
LINDSTROM	1924-36	5,611	1,747	301	81	103	84	98.8%	.311	70	.495/110%
B. ROBINSON	1955-77	10,654	2,848	482	68	268	28	92.0%	.267	52	.471/108%
BOGGS	1982-93	6,773	2,267	448	48	87	16	112.4%	.335	422	.497/108%
TRAYNOR	1920-37	7,559	2,416	371	164	58	158	102.0%	.320	71	.475/106%
KELL	1943-57	6,702	2,054	385	50	78	51	102.9%	.306	106	.460/105%
J. COLLINS	1895-08	6,796	2,000	353	116	65	194	104.9%	.294	147	.455/104%

few players at the hot corner. I'll work with ten on the short list.

The offensive rankings were studied in chapter two but, as noted only Schmidt and Mathews made the Top Fifty list for EBA. Above I present a table of the EBA/<u>A</u>/N which is the adjusted EBA and the percent ahead of the league average during the player's career. As you can see, only four players are well above average and, of them, only Schmidt and Mathews were exceptional sluggers.

DEFENSE

The defensive performance was reviewed in chapter three, and the key indicators are presented in the table on page 120. As noted earlier, assists account for the majority of plays at third base, and so assists per game (A/G) is the key statistic here. All four categories are useful however. In the table on page 120, you can see the clear dominance of Brooks Robinson, strong in every category and an overwhelming lead in range, quickness, headiness and sureness of glove and arm. The best ever.

Percentage Comparison of Fielding Stats of Final Third Base Candidates Compared to the Average Player of the Time

PLAYER	FA MINUS LEAGUE AVER.	PO/G DIVIDED BY LEAGUE AVER.	A/G DIVIDED BY LEAGUE AVER.	DP/G DIVIDED BY LEAGUE AVER.
B. ROBINSON	+.021	+11%	+21%	+31%
SCHMIDT	+.002	+1%	+25%	+25%
J. COLLINS	+.016	+14%	+9%	+7%
BAKER	+.003	+14%	+3%	+22%
BRETT	–.002	+11%	+20%	+10%
BOGGS	+.007	+5%	+8%	+21%
MATHEWS	+.006	+11%	+11%	+3%
KELL	+.015	+11%	+4%	–3%
LINDSTROM	+.009	–4%	0%	–4%
TRAYNOR	–.003	+15%	–1%	–7%

OPINIONS

Pie Traynor took all the honors for the first fifty years of baseball, just ahead of Jimmy Collins. Pie also got the Centennial Team nod. However, the back half of the century has moved a few players mighty close to him. Brooks Robinson has challenged him in the fifties and sixties, and then came Mike Schmidt. Mike wasn't around for most polls, so I couldn't award him the fourth star. But he will clearly earn it, starting with this book! Look in chapter four for more detailed analysis of the opinion polls and surveys.

FIRST TEAM

Perhaps more than with any other position, the classic confrontation of offense against defense is raised here. Brooks Robinson dominated third base defensively like no one else ever! His diving leaps, smothering erstwhile doubles, are etched in the fans' memories. And it's due only to his glove that the opinion polls have given him a strong second place. But these polls were generally taken before the end of Mike Schmidt's career, and there can be little real question that the

Mike Schmidt

Pie Traynor

Final Third Base Ranking

STAR RANKING	OFFENSIVE RANKING	DEFENSIVE RANKING	A CONSENSUS OF THE OPINION
****		1. B. ROBINSON	1. TRAYNOR
***	1. MATHEWS	2. SCHMIDT	2. B. ROBINSON
	2. SCHMIDT	3. J. COLLINS	3. SCHMIDT
			4. J. COLLINS
**	3. BAKER	4. BAKER	5. BRETT
	4. BRETT	5. BRETT	6. MATHEWS
	5. LINDSTROM	6. BOGGS	
	6. BOGGS	7. MATHEWS	
*	7. B. ROBINSON	8. KELL	7. BAKER
	8. TRAYNOR	9. LINDSTROM	8. BOGGS
	9. KELL	10. TRAYNOR	9. KELL
	10. J. COLLINS		10. LINDSTROM

all-time best third sacker in history is Mike Schmidt. Mike certainly had a great glove, not quite as good as Brooks's, but very close. More important, our rules for third base give a strong edge to batting over defense, and Brooks had only a barely above-average bat. That is just not good enough for the best ever. Eddie Mathews had a thin offensive lead over Schmidt in our rankings, but his glove was not exceptional and so he quickly loses the presumption. The polls back me up, too. Schmidt's three MVP awards, ten Gold Gloves, 548 home runs and .608 EBA fit precisely the balance of offense and defense needed at third base. He was durable, steady, got on base a lot, and drove in runs by the bucket. His lead is secure for now, though not as secure as that of Ruth, Gehrig or Walter Johnson.

SECOND TEAM

This is a tougher call. Brooks Robinson was fabulous on defense, but couldn't hit with the greats, batting a relatively feeble .267. His 268 homers helped to rank him a bit above average offensively, but it's not enough. We need power at third.

Eddie Mathews was way out in front of the pack on batting. My star system has Eddie two levels higher on offense, yet Brooks is two levels higher on defense. I see it as a close call. My rules would favor batting at third base, but we also look to opinion rankings in close cases, and I also hear loud and clear the voices of fans and players who resoundingly have favored Brooks. My rules are to let the opinions break ties, and so Brooks Robinson will get the second team position. I expect I'll hear some disagreement on this one!

Chapter Ten

Dream Team Catchers

My favorite people in all of baseball! Johnny Evers and Hugh Fullerton spoke of old-time catcher George Gibson in their book, *Touching Second*: "At one time he had black and blue marks imprinted by nineteen foul tips upon his body, a damaged hand, a bruise on his hip six inches square where a thrown bat had struck, and three spike cuts. Yet he had not missed a game and was congratulating himself on his 'luck.' " I love catchers!

There are eleven catchers in the Hall of Fame. We're all familiar with Johnny Bench, Yogi Berra, Mickey Cochrane and Roy Campanella. Bench and Cochrane each won a couple of MVPs, Campy and Berra won three, and Berra was seven times among the top five in MVP voting. Bill Dickey was rated pretty equally with Cochrane as the best catcher for the first fifty years. Gabby Hartnett and Ernie Lombardi each got one MVP. No catcher made the Top Fifty Hitters list, either in EBA or batting runs. Catchers beat up their knees, which means they usually just don't have enough speed to lift their numbers up closer to the great hitters.

With catchers we look for hitting, obviously. On defense a key is assists, which measure bunt-scrambling ability and also the strength and accuracy of arm to shoot would-be base stealers. Unfortunately, the catchers with the greatest arms don't always score high in assists since the runners just don't run on them! *Steals against* would be a great stat, but it's not available. Catching pop-ups is another good measure, but the putouts statistic has the pitcher's strikeouts crammed into it too, so it's useless for catchers. Thus, we will need to rely on opinion more than with the other positions. The real intangible is the catcher's ability to control the pitcher and keep him in a good rhythm and frame of mind. We can't measure that empirically.

Let's look at the hitting first. I'll do all eleven Hall of Famers and throw in Gary Carter and Carlton Fisk, who are the best the past ten years has seen.

OFFENSE

PLAYER	YEARS	AB	H	2B	3B	HR	SB	PARK EFF.	BA	BR/A	EBA/A/N
EWING	1880-97	5,363	1,625	250	178	71	354	93.9%	.303	197	.552/126%
DICKEY	1928-46	6,300	1,969	343	72	202	36	91.0%	.313	247	.537/122%
BERRA	1946-65	7,555	2,150	321	49	358	30	94.0%	.285	238	.527/121%
BENCH	1967-83	7,658	2,048	381	24	389	68	101.5%	.267	259	.531/121%
CAMPANELLA	1948-57	4,205	1,161	178	18	242	25	102.0%	.276	139	.558/121%
COCHRANE	1925-37	5,169	1,652	333	64	119	64	102.0%	.320	244	.555/119%
HARTNETT	1922-41	6,432	1,912	396	64	236	28	106.0%	.297	234	.542/118%
BRESNAHAN	1897-15	4,481	1,252	218	71	26	212	100.4%	.279	169	.503/117%
CARTER	1974-92	7,971	2,092	371	31	324	39	97.6%	.262	158	.498/112%
FISK	1969-93	8,756	2,356	421	50	376	128	104.7%	.269	194	.502/110%
LOMBARDI	1931-47	5,855	1,792	277	27	190	8	98.0%	.306	191	.469/109%
FERRELL	1929-47	6,028	1,692	324	45	28	29	104.4%	.281	−14	.448/ 95%
SCHALK	1912-29	5,306	1,345	199	49	11	176	98.0%	.253	−103	.402/ 92%

Buck who? Ewing clearly had the most earned bases per at bat after adjusting for the park effect and the league average during his time. He is a bit lower on the sabermetric formula, largely, I think, because of the low weight the stat gives to stolen bases, and also due to his fewer at bats. We all know how important stolen bases were in the dead-ball days, particularly without sluggers to regularly clear the bases. Steals were at the heart of the game. How could the sabermetricians reduce dead-ball steals to the lower weight of today's steals? My EBA formula doesn't get so over-fancy, and that's why I like it better. It says a base is a base, not a fraction. Ewing's speed got him a lot of triples and inside-the-park homers, and each base back then was earned the old-fashioned way. It's wrong to

Percentage Comparison of Fielding Stats of Final Catcher Candidates Compared to the Average Player of the Time

The defensive stats are set forth in chapter three. I'll bring the key analysis up here for ease of review.

PLAYER	FA MINUS LEAGUE AVER.	A/G DIVIDED BY LEAGUE AVER.
EWING	+.018%	+15.7%
CARTER	+.007%	+24.9%
HARTNETT	+.006%	+19.9%
FERRELL	+.005%	+21.1%
DICKEY	+.009%	+8.4%
BENCH	+.006%	+5.4%
BERRA	+.006%	+3.9%
SCHALK	+.009%	+2.0%
CAMPANELLA	+.005%	+2.9%
LOMBARDI	EVEN	+6.2%
COCHRANE	+.007%	−0.7%
BRESNAHAN	+.003%	−7.8%

subject Ewing and his contemporaries to a formula calculated during the day of the slugger, and beg the question by writing off baseball's early days. So I won't.

Look back to chapter three for defensive details, particularly the number of times each player led the league, and the number of Gold Gloves.

Keep in mind that the batting ranking is a comparison to all hitters, in all positions, and so catchers are usually not in the top categories. On defense, however, we rate only against other catchers. I think this approach gives a much better perspective.

OPINION

The polls found no clear favorite, as I reported in detail in chapter four. I have Cochrane, Dickey, Bench, Berra and Ewing, in that order, neck and neck for opinion honors.

FIRST TEAM

So, who is Buck Ewing? I asked myself the same question. I found out that Ewing is one of the best reasons why we should not turn our heads from the players of the 1880s. Mike Shatzkin's *The Ballplayers* said, "Ewing had been baseball's best catcher and, according to his contemporaries, was unequalled as an all-around player in the nineteenth century . . . the catcher on virtually everyone's all time team . . . a master at throwing out baserunners, also a dead ball era home run champ." Bill James cited an article in the 1919 *Reach Guide* which placed Ewing, Cobb and Wagner in the same class, and called Ewing the best! There were many other opinions during the first fifty years of baseball which held Buck to be number one. Recent pollsters have completely forgotten about Old Buck; he doesn't show up anymore at all. But while many of Ewing's contemporaries said he was the best all-around ballplayer of his time, no modern analyst says that of Johnny Bench. My stats have Buck leading on EBA and defense, and what more can a man do? For his time, he was farther ahead of the game than anyone since, and that's the rule we set for evaluating who is on the team. I've got to honor the numbers, and put the great Buck Ewing behind the plate.

SECOND TEAM

It's close between Dickey, Berra and Bench. I'm skipping Campy; he played just nine years before his injury and likely would not have maintained his EBA in his senior years anyway. Dickey has the highest "percent ahead of his time" EBA average, but I can't fit a dime between Dickey, Berra and Bench's offensive contributions, particularly after we neutralized the lousy park effect on Dickey and Berra, pulling them up a whisker over Bench.

Dickey also had the best defensive stats of the three, for what they are worth, although I certainly must let Bench's twelve Gold Gloves challenge that edge.

The pollsters have given Cochrane the nod in a close race, but I think Dickey's numbers are a hair better. I'm going with the numbers here; there are not enough opinions favoring Cochrane to overcome the presumption of Dickey's hair lead. Looking down the list I notice Carter and Hartnett, both with

Final Catcher Ranking

STAR RATING	OFFENSIVE RANKING	DEFENSIVE RANKING	A CONSENSUS OF THE OPINIONS
****		1. EWING	
		2. CARTER	
		3. HARTNETT	
***	1. EWING	4. BENCH	1. COCHRANE
		5. BERRA	2. DICKEY
		6. CAMPANELLA	3. BENCH
		7. DICKEY	4. BERRA
		8. SCHALK	5. EWING
**	2. DICKEY	9. FERRELL	6. HARTNETT
	3. BERRA	10. COCHRANE	7. BRESNAHAN
	4. BENCH	11. LOMBARDI	
	5. CAMPANELLA		
	6. COCHRANE		
	7. HARTNETT		
	8. BRESNAHAN		
	9. CARTER		
*	10. LOMBARDI	12. BRESNAHAN	8. CARTER
	11. FERRELL		9. CAMPANELLA
	12. SCHALK		10. SCHALK
			11. LOMBARDI
			12. FERRELL

more impressive defensive numbers. However, Carter's bat was nearly a whole level below Dickey, and Hartnett is quite close but doesn't have enough steam or reputation to overtake Dickey. Bill James makes an impassioned plea for Berra, but the defense is just not there. So my second team selection goes to Bill Dickey. I'll give Mickey Cochrane an honorable mention.

William "Buck" Ewing

Bill Dickey

Chapter Eleven

Dream Team Pitchers

Pitchers are a different breed of ballplayer. They are the elite of baseball. When I coached, pitchers were the ones I had to "handle" the most, trying to keep them together. It's the position most affected by nerves and emotions.

I said before that hitting is the essence of baseball, its soul. And defense will keep you in a game. But there is just no doubt that pitching is what *wins* games. At any level, you just don't win without pitching. Some pitchers win by blowing the ball by you, as Bob Feller did. Others strike fear in your heart with exploding fastballs, as Nolan Ryan does. And some were masters of control and off-speed pitching, as was Christy Mathewson. The last are my favorites: "garbage pitchers" I call them. I had such a kid, named Eric, on my twelve-year-old Little League team in 1979, and we won it all.

Actually, we don't need to spend a lot of time figuring out how to pick the best pitchers ever. They are not expected to be hitters, certainly not where the DH rule is in effect (and it is for this team). Fielding is a plus, but not a significant factor. We expect pitchers to stop runs from scoring. More than strikeouts, more than holding hitters to a low batting average, more than won-lost records, *the best measure of a pitcher is the number of earned runs he gives up per game.* A pitcher may walk a good hitter, he may let a slapsticker put the ball in play and hope for a defensive out, but he never wants a run to score. The best measure of a pitcher, the one essential thing he is most individually responsible for, is earned runs. And this is a statistic we have always had.

Of course, as with batters, pitchers are affected by the park in which they most pitched, so this effect needs to be factored in. Also, as with batters, pitchers' stats will vary depending on the rules of the times, the field conditions of the different eras of baseball, and the different expectations of an evolving game. So we will normalize the stats against league averages, to see how much lower a pitcher's earned run average (ERA) was in comparison to his times.

As in hitting, there is a sabermetric formula to measure pitchers' performances. It's called *pitching runs*, and is also based on ERA. But it seems to be affected by longevity, as is its counterpart *batting runs*. How, I'm not exactly sure, but it is a cumulative stat. (This is the problem with some of these new stats, you just can't get your arms around them without an advanced stats degree.) Also, it is an *estimated* statistic, and that's where I turn away. Still, I've included the stat for those who like it.

My approach is to calculate the park effect for each pitcher in the same manner as was done for hitters in chapter two. I basically find the *runs factor* for each park, which is the percentage difference between runs scored in one park as opposed to the average of all other parks. Then, since a pitcher plays about half his games in his home park, I halve that percentage. However, since opposing pitchers were able to pitch, on average, one out of seven games in that park (assuming here an eight-team league), I then take six-sevenths of the result. This is the park effect.

For instance, Walter Johnson pitched in Griffith Stadium in Washington from 1907 to 1927. His lifetime ERA was 2.17. Griffith was quite a pitcher's park and produced 7.2 percent fewer runs than the league's other parks during those years (accounting for the slight difference when it was rebuilt after a fire in 1911). Thus the park effect, or runs factor, was 7.2 percent. However, Johnson played only half his games in that park, so his earned run average was helped by only half of 7.2 percent, or 3.6 percent, which means his ERA would have been 3.6 percent higher if he had pitched in the "average park" for his entire career. Now, all the other pitchers got to play one-seventh of their road games in Griffith Park, and Johnson should get the same benefit. Thus, I further reduce the 3.6 percent by one-seventh, which finally gives us the park effect multiplier of 3.1 percent. Thus, Walter Johnson's park effect is 3.1 percent × 2.17 or 0.067. I add this to his 2.17 ERA to yield an adjusted ERA of 2.24. The league ERA for the years he played was 3.31, and so Johnson's ERA was 32.3 percent better (that is, lower) than the league average. In recent years, more teams have meant that opposing pitchers get fewer chances to play in opposing parks. I factor that in accordingly.

It's important to keep in mind that these numbers are just that, numbers. There could be some inaccuracy in how stats were compiled; there could be debate about how far to go to refine them. Different approaches may yield slightly different numbers, and so we need to look at the whole picture.

I believe my adjusted ERA, when compared to the league average, gives us a pretty good estimate of the relative effectiveness of pitchers. As with the adjusted EBA (earned bases average) for hitters, it creates a presumption that one pitcher is better than another. But that is all it does. We then need to compare more deeply the "near neighbors," the pitchers ranked next to each other, to make a final conclusion.

In my charts, I also have included data on team defense, since this statistic helps us understand whether a given ERA was helped more or less by the defensive ability of the fielders. This stat estimates the number of wins produced by the defense above and beyond what the average defense would have done. It follows the approach recommended by Thorn and Palmer for this purpose. Then there are season records, strikeout ratios, and opponents' batting averages which help to clear up any close contests. Next to the pitcher's winning percentage, I have listed the percentage point difference between the pitcher's won-lost average and that of the team's other pitchers. For instance, Walter Johnson's .599 winning percentage was 139 points higher than the .460 mark achieved by Johnson's team when he *wasn't* pitching, over his entire career. I have included pitcher defensive ability and batting average, but they don't weigh in too much.

First we'll look at the raw numbers. After that we'll revisit what the opinions and polls say about the pitchers and choose our first team. We need four pitchers on the roster, but don't worry, I won't cop out. I'll rank all four, and say who was the best ever.

One quick note is regarding a few names *not* on the list. Warren Spahn, Bob Feller and Jim Palmer are often listed among the greatest pitchers ever. However, all three pitched in pitcher's parks. Spahn did his pitching at Braves Field in Boston and County Stadium in Milwaukee, both of which produced fewer than 90 percent of the average runs expected. Feller pitched nearly half of his home games in Municipal Stadium in Cleveland, with a runs factor of only 77 percent. Palmer's park effect was 93 percent. These pitchers' adjusted ERAs are all well above their career averages, so they failed to make the top twenty-five pitchers.

OPINIONS

As noted in chapter four, the survey of five hundred sportswriters in 1950, and the subsequent selection by the All-America Board, named six hurlers: Walter Johnson, Christy Mathewson, Cy Young, Grover Cleveland Alexander, Bob "Lefty" Grove and Carl Hubbell. The *Players' Choice* survey picked Sandy Koufax, Grove, Johnson and Bob Feller. The 1969 Centennial Team picks were Johnson, Grove, Mathewson and Koufax.

Probably the best poll in the last fifty years has been the voting for the Cy Young Award, which began in 1956. Only five players have dominated the votes over its thirty-six-year history (the parentheses include the number of each pitcher's wins followed by the number of years the player received *any* votes): Steve Carlton (four, six); Tom Seaver (three, ten); Jim Palmer (three, eight); Sandy Koufax (three, four); Bob Gibson (two, four); and Roger Clemens (three, six). Note that Koufax won his three awards before a winner was named in *each* league (that began in 1967). And that Clemens has received votes in an incredible six of his first seven years! Twelve pitchers have received the MVP since it was instituted. Hubbell and Newhouser each got two. And while Bob Feller never got one, he was among the top five in vote-getters five times; similarly, Spahn got into the top five vote four times.

In chapter four we took all the polls into consideration and awarded four stars to Johnson, Mathewson, Koufax and

THE TOP TWENTY-FIVE PITCHERS OF ALL TIME

PLAYER	YEARS	TEAM	W L	PCT./ ABOVE TEAM	IP	SH	HR	BB	SO
1. Roger CLEMENS	1984-93	BOS	163-86	.655/.138	2,223	35	145	619	2,033
2. Lefty GROVE	1925-41	PHI/BOS	300-141	.680/.125	3,940	35	163	1,187	2,266
3. Walter JOHNSON	1907-27	WAS	417-279	.599/.139	5,923	110	97	1,362	3,509
4. Hoyt WILHELM	1952-72	NY/CHI	143-122	.540/.011	2,254	5	150	778	1,610
5. Pete ALEXANDER	1911-30	PHI/CHI	373-208	.642/.140	5,189	90	164	951	2,198
6. Ed WALSH	1904-17	CHI	195-126	.607/.097	2,964	57	22	617	1,736
7. Mordecai BROWN	1903-16	CHI	239-130	.648/.063	3,172	45	19	364	1,375
8. Rube WADDELL	1897-10	PHI	193-144	.573/.048	2,961	50	37	803	2,316
9. Sandy KOUFAX	1955-66	LA	165-87	.655/.111	2,324	40	204	817	2,396
10. C. MATHEWSON	1900-16	NY	373-188	.665/.106	4,781	79	91	844	2,502
11. Harry BRECHEEN	1940-53	STL	135-92	.591/.011	1,907	25	117	536	901
12. John CLARKSON	1882-94	CHI/BOS	328-178	.648/.053	4,536	37	161	1,191	1,978
13. Whitey FORD	1950-67	NY	236-106	.690/.103	3,170	50	228	1,086	1,956
14. Kid NICHOLS	1890-06	BOS	361-208	.634/.041	5,057	48	156	1,268	1,868
15. Cy YOUNG	1890-11	CLE/BOS	511-316	.618/.125	7,354	76	138	1,219	2,800
16. Dizzy DEAN	1930-47	STL/CHI	150-83	.644/.107	1,966	26	95	458	1,155
17. Amos RUSIE	1889-01	NY	245-124	.585/.064	3,769	30	76	1,704	1,934
18. Carl HUBBELL	1928-43	NY	253-154	.622/.078	3,590	36	227	725	1,677
19. Hal NEWHOUSER	1939-55	DET	207-128	.580/.051	2,993	33	137	1,249	1,796
20. Stan COVELESKI	1912-28	CLE	215-142	.602/.053	3,082	38	66	802	981
21. Tom SEAVER	1967-86	NY/CIN	311-205	.603/.119	4,782	61	380	1,390	3,640
22. Bob GIBSON	1959-75	STL	251-174	.591/.075	3,884	56	251	1,336	3,117
23. Goose GOSSAGE	1972-93	CHI/NY/SD	121-107	.531/.007	1,760	0	113	717	1,471
24. Sal MAGLIE	1945-58	NY	119-62	.657/.060	1,723	25	169	562	862
25. Nig CUPPY	1892-01	CLE	162-98	.623/.034	2,284	9	62	609	504

SO/BB	OAV	PR/A	ERA	PARK EFFECT	LEAGUE ERA	PCT. AHEAD OF HIS TIMES	ASSISTS PER INN.	BA	TEAM DEFENSE
3.28	.227	320	2.94	114%	4.16	**34%**	.096	.000	−0.7
1.90	.255	643	3.06	108%	4.43	**33%**	.183	.148	10.3
2.58	.227	662	2.17	93%	3.31	**32%**	.228	.235	0.2
2.07	**.216**	289	2.52	96%	3.73	**31%**	.166	.088	−2.1
2.31	.250	522	2.56	109%	3.53	**31%**	.273	.209	3.1
2.81	.218	270	1.82	94%	2.76	**30%**	.407	.193	23.3
2.04	.232	283	2.06	101%	2.92	**30%**	.266	.206	15.4
2.88	.228	248	2.16	103%	2.96	**28%**	.250	.161	−2.7
2.93	**.205**	221	2.76	100%	3.78	**27%**	.098	.097	3.5
2.96	.236	403	2.13	97%	2.94	**27%**	.314	.215	−3.7
1.68	.242	205	2.92	106%	3.85	**26%**	.197	.192	11.8
1.66	.241	477	2.81	111%	3.58	**25%**	.252	.219	−3.2
1.80	.235	315	2.75	91%	3.82	**25%**	.199	.173	7.2
1.47	.250	**653**	2.95	106%	3.84	**25%**	.203	.266	27.3
2.30	.252	**819**	2.63	103%	3.46	**25%**	.267	.210	−0.7
2.52	.253	198	3.03	109%	3.86	**24%**	.144	.225	7.3
1.14	.234	381	3.07	101%	4.03	**24%**	.232	.247	−22.5
1.42	.239	306	3.06	105%	3.87	**23%**	.204	.201	9.9
2.31	.251	248	2.98	97%	3.91	**23%**	.229	.191	10.0
1.22	.262	276	2.89	103%	3.67	**22%**	.276	.159	3.4
2.62	.226	411	2.86	98%	3.67	**21%**	.145	.156	14.3
2.33	.228	335	2.91	103%	3.62	**21%**	.125	.206	−0.5
2.05	.228	147	2.98	94%	3.81	**20%**	.103	.106	5.9
1.53	.245	160	3.15	97%	3.91	**19%**	.163	.135	−0.1
0.83	.275	239	3.48	106%	4.16	**18%**	.242	.233	21.4

LEAGUE LEADERS, AWARDS AND FEATS

| PLAYER | NUMBER OF TIMES LED LEAGUE | | | | | | TRIP CRWN | MVP | CY YOUNG | NO HITS | CS WINS |
	PCT	CG	SH	SO	ERA	OAV					
1. Roger CLEMENS	1	2	3	1	2	3	0	1	3	0	14
2. Lefty GROVE	3	4	3	7	9	1	2	1	NA	0	16
3. Walter JOHNSON	0	6	7	12	5	5	3	1	NA	1	16
4. Hoyt WILHELM	1	0	0	0	2	0	0	0	0	1	14
5. Pete ALEXANDER	0	6	7	6	4	3	4	NA	NA	0	
6. Ed WALSH	1	0	3	2	2	1	0	NA	NA	1	
7. Mordecai BROWN	0	2	2	0	1	1	0	NA	NA	1	
8. Rube WADDELL	1	1	0	7	2	2	1	NA	NA	0	
9. Sandy KOUFAX	1	2	3	4	5	7	3	1	3	4	
10. C. MATHEWSON	1	2	4	5	5	0	2	NA	NA	2	13
11. Harry BRECHEEN	2	0	2	1	1	0	0	NA	NA	0	
12. John CLARKSON	1	3	2	3	1	0	1	NA	NA	0	13
13. Whitey FORD	3	1	2	0	2	0	0	0	1	0	12
14. Kid NICHOLS	0	0	3	0	0	1	0	NA	NA	0	
15. Cy YOUNG	2	3	7	2	2	1	1	NA	NA	3	13
16. Dizzy DEAN	1	3	2	4	0	0	0	0	NA	0	
17. Amos RUSIE	0	1	4	5	2	4	0	NA	NA	0	
18. Carl HUBBELL	1	1	1	1	3	1	0	2	NA	1	16
19. Hal NEWHOUSER	1	2	1	2	2	3	1	2	NA	1	
20. Goose GOSSAGE	0	0	0	0	0	0	0	0	0	0	
21. Stan COVELESKI	1	0	2	1	2	2	0	NA	NA	1	13
22. Tom SEAVER	3	1	2	5	3	3	0	0	3	1	
23. Bob GIBSON	1	1	4	1	1	1	0	1	2	1	15
24. Sal MAGLIE	1	0	1	0	1	1	0	0	NA	1	
25. Nig CUPPY	0	0	1	0	0	0	0	NA	NA	0	

Grove, in that order. Three stars were given to Alexander, Young, Feller, Hubbell, Spahn and Carlton. Clemens has not been aboard long enough for any polls, but his incredible Cy Young Award recognition, winning the award three times, and receiving votes in six of his first seven years, warrants a third star also.

Records. Finally, we have some astounding records set by pitchers. I'm going to mention only the lifetime records because, while there are many amazing single-game or single-season records, this book is about the long run. That's the test of greatness! The Triple Crown of pitching is to achieve the most wins, strikeouts and lowest ERA in a season. Johnson, Alexander and Koufax each did it three times, and Mathewson, Grove and Gomez did it twice. Cy Young won an incredible 511 games in his long career. Nolan Ryan has pitched an astounding seven no-hitters, and his all-time record for career strikeouts is 5,714! Ryan is number one in fewest hits allowed per game and lowest opponents' average (Koufax is second in both categories). Walter Johnson has the most shutouts at 110. While the record for consecutive wins is nineteen, several of our contenders had sixteen in a row (Johnson, Grove and Hubbell), and two had fifteen (Gibson, Carlton).

FIRST TEAM

As I indicated earlier, the adjusted and normalized ERA creates a presumptive rank which other pitchers must somehow overcome with other stats.

Roger Clemens tops the list, but he has been around only ten years as of this writing. He is amazing, but can't hold onto first place. Walter Johnson's lifetime ERA was 2.17, but it was 1.64 after *his* first nine years, which is well ahead of Clemens's pace. "The Rocket" simply needs more time to be in contention for numero uno. But I'm not going to ignore Clemens.

The next two names on the list are Lefty Grove and Walter Johnson. One of them is the best ever, and their comparison creates one of the great all-time debates. Bill James asked: "What argument, if any could be presented against the proposition that Lefty Grove was the greatest pitcher who ever lived?" James noted that Grove led the league in ERA and in winning percentage significantly more times than anyone else

Walter Johnson

Robert "Lefty" Grove

(although Palmer and Thorn dispute James's assertion that Grove led his league in winning percentage five times, they record only three). But, Walter Johnson led the league in strikeouts twelve times to Grove's seven, six times led in complete games to Grove's zero, and five times led in lowest opponents' batting average to Grove's one. Johnson won three Triple Crowns to Grove's two. But the most compelling answer to Bill James's question is that while the two are mighty close indeed, Johnson pitched two thousand more innings than Grove. To my mind, end of argument! The best pitcher ever was Walter Johnson. I just can't imagine what he'd have done if he had possessed a great curveball, but that fastball must have been something to behold! Johnson is nearly everyone's favorite for this honor. His 2.58 strikeout-to-walks ratio, .227 opponents' batting average, 2.17 ERA, sixteen consecutive victories, .599 winning percentage (which is an incredible 139 points higher than the rest of his team), and an all-time record 110 shutouts are compelling evidence—and he compiled them all with a team of only average defensive ability. That he had a reputation for being a great human being is icing on the cake. We'll need his leadership with guys like Grove on the team.

I'll go with Lefty Grove in the number-two slot in the rotation. Only he and Johnson were in the top four in both adjusted ERA and opinion polls. He is another great winner with an awesome .680 percent (125 points higher than the rest of the team's average), two Triple Crown seasons, sixteen consecutive wins, an unsurpassed nine league ERA championships, and seven league strikeout leads. Reputed to be a most unfriendly guy, he was surely a terror to hitters. He once struck out Ruth, Gehrig and Bob Meusel on nine pitches, with the winning run on third; another day he relieved with the bases full and struck out Ruth, Gehrig and Tony Lazzeri on ten pitches. Well, he may have been an angry guy, but he won, and that gets him on the team.

I'll start Clemens third. He has the ERA presumption, and he has backed it up. He has not been around long enough to win a place on the opinion polls, but he'll be there, starting with this book! He got Cy Young votes in six of his first seven years, and won it outright three times. He's got an MVP, and an unmatched 3.28 strikeout-to-walk ratio. Opponents bat just .227 against him, and he gets all of this done pitching in the best hitter's park in baseball with a good, but not overpowering team behind him. He slipped a bit in 1993, going 11-14 with a 4.46 ERA. Let's see how he rebounds.

For the last first-team spot, I could go a few ways. I'm passing on Hoyt Wilhelm because he has not earned a place on anyone else's list. He never scored among the top ten in MVP voting, and never got even one Cy Young vote. He's got a great ERA, but this knuckleballing reliever is not an all-timer in my book. If I were going to put a reliever on the team, I'd go for Goose Gossage, or Rollie Fingers. But I'm not looking for a reliever. I know that they have come a long way from the days when they were the defensive equivalent of pinch hitters, but they have not come far enough. Even today, it's still generally a demotion to the bullpen.

We'll look at Pete Alexander for sure, but there are a few guys only a percent or two behind him in adjusted ERA who also deserve a look. I'll skip over Ed Walsh too. Big Ed had the lowest lifetime ERA of all time, and won forty games in 1908, but, the handsome coal miner threw a spitter, perhaps the greatest spitter in history, but that was all he had. He was passed over by the 1950 poll, and has not been named since. The spitter is an outlawed pitch and, without anything else, he doesn't make this team.

So, besides Alexander that leaves us with Sandy Koufax, Rube Waddell, Mordecai Brown and Christy Mathewson. Waddell was great, but was not wrapped too tightly. Connie Mack, his manager, lamented about what could have been, but he just couldn't get the big kid to be all he could be. You were never sure whether he'd show up or go play sandlot ball with kids instead. His winning percentage was only .573, and only .048 higher than the rest of his team. He was passed over by the 1950 vote. Rube was truly a wonder, but hasn't enough to overcome the adjusted ERA presumption of those above him on the list.

"Three Finger" Mordecai Brown lost half of his middle finger and paralyzed his pinkie in his father's corn shredder. The accident gave him a natural knuckleball. But there is little beyond his record 1.04 ERA in 1905 to move him up the list.

Roger Clemens

Grover Alexander

His winning percentage was only sixty-three points higher than the rest of his team's and his strikeout-to-walk ratio was low compared to the others here. He wasn't considered one of the very best by his own era, and will be passed here.

So, it's Alexander, Koufax or Mathewson. Christy Mathewson was an all-time opinion favorite, but he doesn't have quite enough to overcome the presumption of the lower adjusted ERAs of the other two. Mathewson did win a pair of Triple Crowns, but Koufax won three and Alexander won four. Alexander and Mathewson traded places from time to time on various "who's the best" lists, although Christy won more times. However, the park effect probably was not figured in, and Pete pitched in Baker Bowl with a 272-foot right field fence close to his left hip. Later, he pitched in Wrigley Field, another batter's park. Christy, on the other hand, enjoyed a pitcher's park at the cavernous Polo Grounds.

And then there were two! It's between Koufax and Alexander. Sandy Koufax is only a few percentage points behind Alexander in lifetime adjusted ERA. Yet, he pitched the best six straight years of baseball ever, from 1961 to 1966. He won three Triple Crowns, boasts an enormous 2.93 strikeout-to-walk ratio, led the league five times in ERA and four times in strikeouts, dominated Cy Young voting during the sixties, won an MVP and twice finished second.

I saw Koufax, and it's hard to believe he's not going to be on the first team, but I think we have to let the rules make the call here. Alexander won a record four Triple Crowns to Koufax's three. Koufax just can't overcome the ERA presumption rule we set out front. Moreover, Sandy pitched during the era of an enlarged strike zone. Pete's wins over the rest of his team is the highest of all time. Hampered by a great hitter's park, he still managed a phenomenal ninety shutouts. He pitched double the innings of Koufax and was effective for all of his twenty seasons. He has earned his place in history. His alcoholism surely held him back, but from what we will never know. I repeat: Alexander won four Triple Crowns, led the league six times in strikeouts, and had an uncanny ability to uncork his sinker when needed, such as the legendary strikeout of Tony Lazzeri in the 1950 World Series . . . in

Sandy Koufax

Christy Mathewson

Cy Young

Carl Hubbell

relief after pitching nine innings the day before at thirty-nine years of age!

What a staff! Walter Johnson, Lefty Grove, Roger Clemens and Grover Cleveland "Pete" Alexander.

SECOND TEAM

I'm still passing over Wilhelm, Walsh and Brown as explained previously. Harry Brecheen is not in the Hall, did not otherwise achieve exceptional stats, and will not be considered further. So, the next candidate pitchers on the list are Rube Waddell, Sandy Koufax, Christy Mathewson, John Clarkson, Whitey Ford, Kid Nichols and Cy Young.

As discussed before, Sandy Koufax and Christy Mathewson could not climb over Pete Alexander, but they certainly hold their ranks here and make the second team. They both easily overcome Waddell.

Final two second-team spots? Well, Waddell has not been a top favorite in the polls, but his awesome 2.88 ratio of strikeouts to walks, his seven years leading the league in strikeouts, his low .228 opponents' batting average, and his Triple Crown are enough to hold onto his rank, and the third spot on the second team.

Clarkson, Ford, Nichols and Young are all tied in adjusted ERA for the final spot on the team. It's a close call. Clarkson won a Triple Crown. Ford's .690 was one of the highest percentage winners of all time, .103 over the other Yankee pitchers of his day. But Cy Young? Well, he *was* Cy Young! He won the most games ever, pitched the most innings, had a great strikeout ratio (led the league seven times), won at a pace of 120 percentage points beyond his team, earned one Triple Crown, and threw three no-hitters! That's good enough for me.

Carl Hubbell made the cutoff for the first-fifty-year team, and is the only pitcher to win two MVP awards (except Hal Newhouser's two during the war years). He won sixteen straight games, had a whopping strikeout-to-walk ratio of 2.88, and a stingy .228 opponents' batting average, all in a hitter's park! However, I don't see it as enough to catch Cy Young. Terrific Tom Seaver is so close behind . . . but not quite close enough.

Satchel Paige

Satchel Paige was regarded by many as the best pitcher ever. We'll never know because the Negro Leagues never kept records. But such a legend deserves more than an Honorable Mention; it's enough that the history of baseball is disgraced as it is with banning men of color. So I'm giving Satchel a fifth spot on this team. Call it what you want, it's my book!

HONORABLE MENTION

Steve Carlton did win a record four Cy Young awards (Clemens will be the next to do it!). Nolan Ryan has that incredible seven no-hitters and holds the all-time strikeout record. I'm exhausted just thinking about these guys!

PART THREE

The All-Time Dream Team: Up Close and Personal

Babe Ruth

The greatest baseball player who ever lived, George Herman "The Babe" Ruth, was born on February 6, 1895, a son of a saloon keeper in the rough waterfront section of Baltimore. According to his autobiography, *The Babe Ruth Story*, young Babe soon became too much to handle, and at the age of seven, the tobacco-chewing "incorrigible" was sent to a reform school. He told Fred Lieb, "I learned early to drink beer, wine, whiskey, and I think I was about five when I first chewed tobacco. There was a lot of cussin' in Pop's saloon, so I learned a lot of swear words, some really bad ones." He stayed at St. Mary's Industrial School, with a few short-lived attempts to go home, until he was nineteen. He was trained to be a tailor, and played catcher on the school team. He was signed by the Baltimore Orioles in 1914 as a pitcher for $600, was soon sold to the Boston Red Sox for $2,900, and played his first major league game that year.

Babe Ruth was not just a pitcher; he was an all-star-class pitcher who won twenty-three games for the Red Sox in both 1916 and 1917. But he also hit some tremendous home runs, so through much of 1918 and into 1919 he pitched every fourth day and played left field the rest of the time. The burden of this got a bit much and Babe stopped pitching. He hit twenty-nine homers in 1919, thirteen more than the American League record. Most fans thought it was a fluke, but he belted fifty-four the next year to settle the debate. He hit over fifty home runs four times, and over forty homers eleven times. His lifetime batting average was .343, his earned bases average was a hefty .719, and his .692 slugging average is an all-time major league record. And much of this occurred in

Babe Ruth

Yankee Stadium, one of the worst "batter's" parks in history.
That he was a feared batter is attested to by his 2,053 walks,
even though the awesome Lou Gehrig batted behind him!
Ruth led the Yankees to ten pennants, and the 1927 Yankees
was considered to be the best major league team ever.

A big part of the Ruth mystique was the public's belief that

he could hit a homer at will. Ruth discusses this in his autobiography. In 1928, in a long tie game he noticed that Ford
Frick's father appeared tired. He pointed to a passing freight
train beyond the fences and said, "I'll end it for you, Pappy."
Then he knocked a homer into the open boxcar. In another
game at the Polo Grounds he belted what he thought was a
homer, but umpire Billy Evans ruled it was an "inch foul."
Ruth bellowed that the next would be an inch fair, and hit
another to the same spot. He looked at Evans who said, "It
was an inch fair. Go ahead, Babe."

Of course, Babe's most written about home run came
against Chicago in the 1932 World Series. The Babe had gotten a lot of abuse from the fans, so when he stepped to the
plate in the fourth inning he pointed to center field. He did
not swing at the first two pitches, and loudly called them
strikes himself, raising one, then two fingers to signify the
count. The fans howled. Then Babe pointed again to the center field bleachers and smacked the next pitch into them.

Babe was one to live life to the fullest off the field. In his autobiography he openly discusses his hard-and-fast lifestyle and
his endless run-ins with manager Miller Huggins, and others
seem to have made a living writing about them. I'll leave it up
to them to judge Babe's actions. But he was always true to the
game, at times playing with a fever so as not to disappoint the
fans. His many exhibition games and countless trips to see kids
in need of a lift are enough to overcome any interest of mine in
whatever he did privately. He played for twenty-one seasons,
and did what he had to do to stay on top of his game.

Ruth was released to the Boston Braves in 1935 and played
only twenty-eight games in what he termed a nightmare. His
legs, even his love of batting, were gone. He thought constantly of quitting. In a last hurrah, a few days before he ended
his career, he momentarily found the old spark and smacked
three home runs, including the only shot ever hit over the
roof at Pittsburgh's Forbes Field.

Babe never got a shot at managing, the dream of his latter
years. It seems his lack of discipline and disregard of rules all
of his career finally caught up to him. He contracted throat
cancer and passed on in 1948.

Willie Mays

The greatest all-around player ever was born on May 6, 1931, in Westfield, Alabama, the first of eleven children. His mother had been a high school track star. His stepdad played semipro ball in his spare time. In his autobiography, *Say Hey!*, Willie Mays says he first played semipro with his dad at age fourteen, and played his first full professional game in the Negro Leagues for the Birmingham Barons at the age of sixteen.

The New York Giants signed Mays at nineteen, and he played a year in the minors. After the start of the 1951 season, manager Leo Durocher called him to New York. Scared about the big leagues, Willie at first refused to go. He told Durocher he didn't think he was ready yet, and didn't think he could hit big-league pitching. Durocher screamed at him for a minute, then asked what he was hitting. Willie answered, ".477."

Willie played his first big-league game on May 25, 1951. He went 0-12 in his first three games. Finally, in his first home game, he got his first hit—a homer to the top of the Polo Grounds' left field roof. The pitcher was Warren Spahn. And so it began. He finished up the year as Rookie of the Year, helped win a pennant, and played against the Yankees in the World Series. Then the army called and a two-year stint in the service interrupted the "Say Hey Kid."

The story of Willie's early years has Leo Durocher in the center. The feisty competitive manager and Willie developed a father/son relationship. Willie called him "Mista Leo." In 1954 when Willie was ahead of Babe Ruth's home run pace and the pressure was mounting, Leo told him not to go for home runs, but to scatter his hits to all fields. Willie won the

Willie Mays

batting title that year with a .345 average, winning the title the last day of the season by breaking a three-way tie with Duke Snider and Don Mueller by going three for four. (Mays hit forty-one homers.) While Durocher always told Mays how good he was and built Willie's confidence, he was also firm. Durocher once benched Mays for a few games because Willie was not hitting enough to right field.

It wasn't all roses for Mays. Durocher was replaced by Bill Rigney in 1956, and Rigney seemed out to overcome the perception that Willie's manager coddled him. Mays hit only .296 that year. Then, in 1958 the team moved to San Francisco. The fans expected Willie to hit sixty-one homers, but he only delivered twenty-nine (with a .347 batting average!). It took five years for Willie to win them over, a curiosity many have yet to figure out.

Willie always played his heart out and hustled at every moment, so much so that several times he drove himself to collapse and exhaustion. "I always played as if every game was the World Series," he said. When he hit forty-nine homers in 1962, leading the Giants to a pennant, San Francisco was his. He hit forty-seven in 1964, and fifty-two in 1965, batting .317.

In 1972, after twenty-one years of baseball, Willie was traded back to New York, to play with the Mets. He was disappointed at first, and the Giants did not handle it well, cavalierly dismissing him. But, the owner of the Mets wanted Willie back in New York. His first hit for the Mets was the same as his first hit for the Giants, a home run.

Lou Gehrig

His teammates affectionately called him "Buster," because of what he did to baseballs, and what the baseballs he hit did to whatever they smashed into. The "Iron Horse" was a steely, muscular man, possessed of a terrifying strength.

Henry Louis Gehrig was born in the Yorkside section of New York City's upper East Side on June 19, 1903, the son of German immigrants. His father was a handyman; his mother, whom he loved dearly, was a domestic worker.

Early on, Lou demonstrated the characteristics that were to mark his later life. The chubby-faced, fat kid never stayed home from school when sick, a trait that led to his greatest achievement in baseball, a record 2,039 straight games without missing one! At the age of eight, he worked odd jobs and brought home his pennies to his mom to help out. He was never in trouble.

He played high school baseball for the High School of Commerce, which won the New York City championship. The fat, clumsy first baseman was only a .200 hitter but showed signs of the power that was to mark his future. When the team traveled to play the Chicago champs, Lou smacked a home run, a feat never before accomplished by a high school player. He returned a hero.

It was football that got him a scholarship, as the coach of Columbia liked what he saw as the big, beefy fullback bulled through the line. Gehrig was converted to tackle and was an average player, leaving to play pro baseball before he finished college. He played a summer under an alias for the Giants, and then signed with the Yankees in 1924 for $1,500. He was

Lou Gehrig

quite clumsy, but he was a slugger. In his first game he charged a bunt and then didn't know what to do with the ball, letting a run score; a few innings later he belted a game-winning homer.

He had his first date as a pro, and soon married Eleanor Twitchell in 1933. He left for the Stadium an hour after the ceremony to play baseball.

The story of Lou Gehrig is a story of determination to succeed. His wife said it poignantly, "No matter what his achievements, he was dogged by a sense of failure and a need, constantly, to prove himself. Success brought Lou no sense of attainment, no relaxation. He was afraid that if he loosened his grip for a moment, everything he had struggled for would slip away from him." Whatever his motivation, Lou worked endlessly to become a better fielder. He was constantly taking extra practice, seeking advice, and bettering his fielding ability until he finally became a decent, if only average, fielder.

Lou was never able to lose his "dunce" reputation. He once gave a live television commercial for a product called "Huskies." When asked, "Tell me Lou, to what do you owe your tremendous hitting strength and fine condition?" he replied, "Wheaties."

Lou's feats on the field are examined in detail elsewhere in this book. But his greatest feat came in the way he handled the disease which slowly sapped his great strength, and too young took his life. Amyotrophic lateral sclerosis came to be known and still is known today, more than fifty years later, as "Lou Gehrig's Disease." He fought it valiantly. The "Iron Horse" had become synonymous with invincibility, but those great legs began to wobble, and balls slipped from a once iron grip. Finally, it was time to say goodbye. In a stirring speech at a packed Yankee Stadium, Gehrig told the crowd, "I may have been given a bad break, but I got an awful lot to live for. I consider myself the luckiest man on the face of the earth."

Honus Wagner

There are only a few players who have regularly been cited as the greatest baseball player of all time — Buck Ewing, back in the 1880s, Ty Cobb, Babe Ruth, maybe Walter Johnson and even Willie Mays. But that's about it. Except for Honus Wagner, who easily joins that list. The great John McGraw said of him, "I consider Wagner not only as the number one shortstop, but had he played in any other position than pitcher he would have been equally great in them. He was the nearest thing to a perfect player. . . ."

The "Flying Dutchman" was born on February 24, 1874, to poor German immigrants. He grew up in Mansfield (now Carnegie), Pennsylvania, fourth in a family of six. He went to work in the coal mines with his father at the age of twelve.

He played town baseball at the age of fifteen, and became one of the best sandlot players in the Pittsburgh area. He played semipro and professional ball for a few years and was signed by the Yankee's Ed Barrow. Harry Kech reported that, "Honus was late in reporting and missed the training period. When asked the reason for the delay, he explained that, since the players did not receive free meals until the season opened, he thought it best to remain at home where he could eat better."

Honus was a right-handed batter who stood 5'11", with huge powerful shoulders, strong arms, great big hands, and a barrel chest, all sitting atop of the two most bowed legs you ever saw. But he could run like the wind. Fred Lieb wrote that, "When he sped to second base on one of his 720 stolen bases, he looked like a hoop rolling down the baselines."

Honus Wagner

He was the original good old boy, mild-mannered, friendly. "How about that!" was the expression he was known by. He was a storyteller who would captivate any audience with baseball stories, whether in the dugout, a saloon (he liked oceans of beer), or out fishing.

Wagner was friendly, but was no patsy. Once the irritable Ty Cobb yelled from first base, "I'm coming down on the first pitch, you krauthead." Cobb was true to his word and came charging into second, feet threateningly high. Wagner took the throw and slammed his mitt into Cobb's face, loosening a few teeth. Honus grinned at Cobb, "We also play a bit rough in this league, Mr. Cobb!"

Honus was also shy. Fred Lieb reported that upon winning his fourth straight batting title in 1909, Honus was invited to a sports banquet at New York's Waldorf Astoria. He replied, "What would I do up there with all those swells? Besides, I ain't got no monkey suit and I ain't going to hire one. I don't make speeches, and let my bat talk for me in the summertime."

And so his bat did talk: eight batting championships, a lifetime batting average of .329, playing until he was forty-four.

An MVP vote on this team would be close, with Willie Mays and Walter Johnson, perhaps even Babe Ruth. But on this All-Time Dream Team, I'll bet Honus Wagner would get my vote!

Nap Lajoie

Napolean Lajoie played wholly within the dead ball era of baseball, which lasted from its 1871 beginning until about 1920, when a more lively ball was introduced. It was a time when infielders reigned supreme, as batsmen poked the ball at the infield gaps and dragged bunts down the line. Lajoie was not only the best infielder in this "time of the infielder," but he was one of the most powerful batters, too, smacking shin-splintering line drives at those who crept in on him.

Nap was born on September 15, 1874, in Woonsocket, Rhode Island. He was the son of French-Canadian farmers, and the eighth of eleven children. He had limited schooling, having instead to work odd jobs such as sweeping floors. He was never able to write. He played ball on dirt streets, and eventually was selected to play semipro for a village team. He was driving a village hack when asked to play for Fall River in the New England League in 1896. That summer the Philadelphia Phillies purchased teammate Phil Geier, and Fall River was so pleased with the offer that they threw in Lajoie. The rest is history. When the American League was formed, Lajoie jumped to the Philadelphia Athletics under Connie Mack, and after the Phillies obtained an injunction against his ever playing in Philadelphia, he was traded to Cleveland. He was never allowed to play in Pennsylvania during the next ten years.

Larry, as he was most often called, Lajoie (pronounced properly as "lazhwa," commonly as "laj-a-way," and wrongly as "lajoy") played in the majors for twenty-one years. Bob Broeg wrote, "He was a handsome fellow, big and dark, with

Napoleon Lajoie

bold features and arresting eyes. He wore his cap cocked on
the side of his head, which was covered with thick, dark, wavy
hair. And the Frenchman wore the uniform roll collar of his
day, slightly turned up to make an attractive frame for his
face. With the flourish of an instinctive artist, he habitually

drew a line in the dust along home plate, a prelude to facing the pitcher."

He was most known for his gracefulness, and is so described on his Hall of Fame plaque. *New York Sun* writer George Trevor wrote, "Every pose was like a picture, yet there was no striving on Lajoie's part for artistic effects. His gracefulness was innate, living poetry, a part of the eye-filling D'Artagnan of the diamond."

But Lajoie was equally known for his searing line drives. It's said he once killed two sparrows with one shot from his bat. Third basemen refused to challenge this great pull hitter in on the grass. His smashes down the left field line were legendary, and his 648 doubles rank among the top ten of all time. One drive in Cleveland hit the center field screen with such force that the outfielder could not extract it.

Lajoie was a popular player. Cleveland made him player/ manager, and nicknamed the team "Naps" after him. Fans went hundreds of miles to see him play. Although the tale has never been proven, it even seems that the St. Louis Browns tried to help him win the batting title in the 1910 race against the hated Ty Cobb. Lajoie collected seven infield hits while the third baseman curiously played him too deep. Cobb won the title, but both players received the coveted Chalmers automobile since their .385 averages were only .0007 apart. An error in the stats discovered forty-three years later had actually deprived Lajoie of the title, although the error has still not been officially corrected.

If there was a chink in Lajoie's armor, it was his lack of great speed, a liability in the dead ball days of baserunning. Yet he put up some great numbers, and was clearly the best all-around second bagger of them all.

Buck Ewing

His epitaph reads, "One of the greatest players in the annals of the game. Ewing was acknowledged to be the best catcher of his day and as an all-around player he has never had a superior, if indeed he has had an equal."

Old Buck was born in Russell Station, outside of Cincinnati, Ohio, on Christmas Day, 1859. He took to baseball as a young lad, surpassing his playmates in the game of one-cat. Later, he had a job as a wagon driver, and played baseball on Sundays. In the fall of 1879, a team of barnstormers stopped off for a game and were quite impressed by Buck's ability. He was signed by Rochester for $85 a month plus board, a princely salary in those days. He later went to the Troy Club of the National League, but played most of his prime for the New York Giants.

Buck's ability behind the plate was enormous. He had the best throwing arm ever behind the plate. He possessed not only great throwing strength, but could throw from any position. Sam Crane wrote of him in the *New York Journal* in 1912, "He was righthanded and got the ball away with remarkable quickness. Frequently, he took no step when throwing, and never threw from over his shoulder or head, but snapped the ball with a sidearm swing that struck the baseman's glove like a lump of lead. He was agile and active as a cat, and could recover balls quicker than any catcher who ever was behind the plate." It was said he would sit on his haunches, perhaps the first catcher ever to do so, and innocently look at the pitcher; then, without moving his head, Ewing would snap the ball to first base to catch the runner unawares with a rifle-shot pickoff.

William "Buck" Ewing

As a batter, again, Buck was one of the best of his era. Crane said, "Ewing was as near to being free of any weaknesses as anyone before the great Ty Cobb. . . . When it came to hitting, Ewing was as good at inside work as any in the country. He was smart, and always studied the different situations presented to him. He not only was a 'heavy' hitter, but could place the ball to a nicety that few other players could approach, batting over .300 nine years in a row." Ewing was the first player to register a double-digit home run total—ten in 1883. He is also credited with hitting the longest ball ever at the Polo Grounds, a wallop over the left field wall near Eighth Avenue, to a spot long marked by a small flag. He topped the league in triples in 1884 with twenty, hitting three in one game. While not a speedster, Buck was quick and bright and so got a good jump on pitchers and was an excellent base stealer. He employed a hook slide to get under many tags. One day he stole second and third, announced he would steal home . . . and did!

To complement his talent, Ewing was a friendly, happy-go-lucky person, and a natural field general. His teammates were inspired by him, and together they were always a merry—and winning—crew. He also had a great ability to get on the umpire's good side. When fans would get riled and begin to get on the ump, Buck would calm them down, saying, "Easy, up there, easy, he's where he can see 'em and you're not."

The ever-popular Ewing managed the Reds and the Giants to end his career. Having invested wisely in real estate, he enjoyed his later years with wife, Anna. After contracting Bright's disease, Ewing died in 1906. Connie Mack, also a catcher during Ewing's time, called Ewing the greatest catcher ever. (He did not vote so in 1950, because players before 1900 were excluded from consideration.) The 1919 *Reach Guide* linked him with Wagner and Cobb as the greatest ballplayers who ever lived. Certainly, Ewing was the best ballplayer before 1900. He received the most votes for the Hall of Fame from the 1936 veterans committee (tied with Cap Anson) and entered the Hall with an Old-Timer vote in 1939. History has nearly forgotten old Buck . . . until now!

Ted Williams

One thing that has amazed me as I wrote this book and got closer to the athletes who were the very best, was how very different they were. Some were happy people, like Honus Wagner and Nap Lajoie; others were miserable, like Ty Cobb, or angry like Lefty Grove. Where does Ted Williams, owner of the all-time perfect swing, fit? Let's hear his own words, from *My Turn at Bat*.

> *I'm glad it's over. Before anything else, understand that I'm glad it's over. I'm so grateful for baseball — and so grateful I'm the hell out of it as a player. . . . I wanted to be the greatest hitter who ever lived. . . . Certainly nobody worked harder at it. It was the center of my heart, hitting a baseball. . . . As a kid I wished it on every falling star: please let me be the hitter I want to be.*

Ted went on to rail against the press, the Boston Red Sox management, the draft laws, and the left center fence in Comiskey Park against which he injured his elbow. Unlike Ty Cobb, who claimed he was misunderstood, Ted's eerily honest admission of his uncontrollable frustration, sensitivity, temperament and "emotional, explosive nature" (his words) touched me deeply. His incredible love for hitting — virtually the only thing he ever wanted to do, practicing for endless hours on the field, practicing his swing for hours in his room, hours on end — reveals a love for the game unmatched by anything I have ever learned about any other player.

Theodore Samuel Williams was born on August 30, 1918, in San Diego's North Park section. His father had a small photography shop and minor bureaucratic jobs before he left

Ted Williams

the family. His mother, May, was a life-long Salvation Army
worker. She was never home, as Ted recalls, constantly working on the streets. It was a continual source of embarrassment

to young Ted and to his father, who eventually divorced his wife. Ashamed by the public spectacle of this domineering mother, never close to his father, Ted was left to fend for himself, so I guess it's not hard to understand the hostility he carried throughout his career. Ted was a child during the Great Depression and, while the family was not impoverished, there was little to go around. Ted drank orange juice, ate potatoes, never went out with girls, was a "lousy" student, and hit baseballs or round oily rags or whatever else he could find, every free moment he had. He even carried his bat to class. Tall, gangly, skinny, and slow as a bunt in mud (he once hit two triples in a game and then got picked off at third both times!), he could never field worth much. But Ted could *hit*.

He signed at age seventeen with the newly formed San Diego Padres of the Pacific Coast League for $150 per month. Bobby Doerr, a teammate, commented "He was something to see, batting balls out of sight." Three years later Ted broke into the majors with the Red Sox for $3,000 per year.

Williams hit the ground running, batting .327 his first year and hitting thirty-one homers to win Rookie of the Year honors. He hit .344 his second year, and in his junior year reached a standard that may never again be seen. Naturally, he did so in the most dramatic fashion possible. Batting .3995 before the last day of the 1941 season, he passed up an offer to sit out the last game and become the first .400 hitter in over a decade. This alone was an heroic attitude, and the consummate hitter backed himself up by going six for eight during the day's doubleheader to end the season with a .406 average.

To have a chance of stopping him, teams shifted their defense to right field, giving up the left side except for one defender. Known as the "Boudreau shift," it was only minimally successful.

What did stop Ted was war. He lost 3½ seasons to World War II, and three more to the Korean War. In Korea, he flew an F-9 Panther jet on thirty-nine missions. On one he was hit by ground fire, losing electricity, hydraulics and instruments. His plane on fire, Williams belly-landed at 200 mph and skidded 5,000 feet before he could escape.

But the memory of Ted the person will be of his running feud with the press and fans of Boston. He was fined several times for spitting toward fans, and once lost control of his bat in a temper tantrum and beaned a sixty-year-old lady.

The better memory, however, is of a truly generous man. Ray Robinson writes in *Ted Williams* that Ted often gave his lunch money to hungrier classmates. He frequently and secretly visited sick or dying kids, and a few times he belted a promised home run for them. He tirelessly worked for the Jimmy Fund for the Children's Cancer Hospital in Boston. In the 1946 World Series, he had his wife give six of his ten tickets for each game to GIs on the streets.

Walter Johnson

He is quite simply the greatest pitcher who ever lived!

Walter Perry Johnson was born on November 6, 1887, to farmers in Humbolt, Kansas. The family sought a better life in Olinda, California, when Walter was fourteen. Already big and strong, Walter played pick-up ball around the local oil fields, and by high school he had trouble finding someone to catch his fireball. He eventually got a summer job pitching town ball in Weiser, Idaho, and working as a posthole digger for the phone company.

In 1907, the owner of the beleaguered Washington Senators got a series of letters from a traveling businessman in the Rocky Mountains about the strikeout king of Idaho's Snake River Valley League. Jack Newcombe reports one letter in *The Fireballers*: "This Walter Johnson has a pitch that is faster than Amos Rusie's and control that is better than Mathewson's. He throws so fast you can't see 'em, and he knows where he's throwing because if he didn't, there would be dead bodies strewn all over Idaho!" Johnson was signed by the last-place Senators for $350 per month.

They called him the classic hayseed. He showed up at the Senators' field in a too-small tweed suit. He didn't smoke or drink, and ate ice cream by the quart. He was a modest man, mild-mannered, friendly and forebearing. These qualities endeared him to legions of fans, and to sportswriters who wrote of his chivalrous nature and dubbed him "The White Knight." Newcombe reports on Johnson's homespun ways when once he and two teammates were on their way to the movies and he stopped for a while to chat with a fan. After

Walter Johnson

a while Walter broke away and explained to his impatient teammates that the fellow said he grew up in Kansas and knew Walter's sister. "I didn't know you had a sister," said one player. "Well, I don't," responded Johnson, "but he was a nice fellow, and I didn't want to be rude to him."

The baseball memory of Johnson will always focus on the quality expressed by his most famous nickname, "The Big Train." He threw so hard and so fast that the ball went by with the *swoosh* of a locomotive, impacting the catcher's mitt with a thunderclap. A big 6'1" right-hander, Johnson threw exploding fastballs with an easy sidearm motion. The Senators had only enough talent to get him into one World Series during his twenty-one seasons, yet Johnson won 416 games (110 by shutout, the most of any pitcher ever). One year he pitched fifty-six consecutive straight scoreless innings. He once got irritated at the New York press for saying he couldn't beat the Yankees. So, after only a day's rest, he went out and shut out the Bronx Bombers. When the papers called it a fluke, Johnson asked for the ball again, and shut them out the next day too. In fact, he shut out the Yankees three times in four days. The papers grew silent!

He is reputed to have pitched the fastest ever. Lefty Grove, the second-best pitcher ever, said of Johnson, "I think Johnson was the greatest I ever saw, and his curve was faster than Feller's fastball." Well, Johnson never had to throw that curve much, he just threw fastballs, one right after the other. He would have been far greater if he had an effective curve, and George Sisler mused that with an off-speed pitch, no one would ever have gotten a hit off Johnson. That batters did get hits was because players got a good toehold on the plate, knowing that Johnson never, but never, threw at batters. He was afraid to hurt anyone!

In 1927 he was hit in the leg by a line shot during practice. He tried to pitch thereafter with an iron brace, but it was over. He managed for a few years, and passed on in 1946.

Lefty Grove

The best left-hander in history, Robert Moses Grove, was born on March 6, 1900, in the Cumberland Mountain town of Lonaconing, Maryland. It was said he was a direct descendant of Betsy Ross. He worked in the soft coal mines for a while, but hated the dirty, backbreaking work, and soon went to work in a glass factory. He is remembered as a standoffish kid with little to say, but he really loved baseball, and went around with his glove hooked onto his belt buckle.

Grove got his first professional chance at age seventeen with a town team in nearby Midland, and later played with the Martinsburg team in the Blue Ridge League of West Virginia. An opposing pitcher became exasperated when Lefty shut out his team twice, and wrote to Jack Dunn of the minor league Baltimore Orioles about how good Lefty was, *just to get him out of the League!* Dunn took a look, and bought Grove's contract for a promise to build the team a new fence. Grove got $300 per month.

Lefty had serious control problems at first. He had only his fastball, and he walked a lot of batters in the minor leagues. Nevertheless, Grove's blazing speed made him virtually unhittable. Dunn refused to sell Grove until he was twenty-five years of age, costing him perhaps as many as one hundred victories. Finally, Grove was sold to the major league Philadelphia Athletics, and Connie Mack had to pay a record $100,600 for him. It was a good buy, because "Old Mose" led the league in strikeouts his first six years and, after an initial period of wildness, settled in to win more than twenty games for seven straight seasons, including an MVP 31-4 season in 1931.

Lefty Grove

Grove was known for his wild tantrums, especially when he lost a game, and he directed his tirades at any player whose error cost him a game. When a teammate misplayed a liner to cost Grove a record seventeenth straight win in 1931, he smashed locker stools, and screamed and hollered. He was known, however, to have enough control over himself to smash walls only with his right hand, and to kick *empty* water buckets!

Grove was a big man, 6'3" and all of 200 pounds. His long, loose arms and his mound stance were models of gracefulness. Jack Newcombe reported in *The Fireballers*: "When he bent forward to get his signal and set his target, he looked as if he were peering intently through a tiny cellar window. Then he flung his arm back, kicked his right leg forward, and cut loose—and the batter had the uncomfortable feeling that Grove was going to jam the ball right down his throat." Mickey Cochrane, a Hall of Famer who caught Grove and hit against Feller, said, "Feller never saw the day when he could throw as fast as Grove. Lefty was bigger, more powerful, and had a smoother delivery. When he let his fastball go, it exploded."

Lefty used that fastball exclusively early in his career. He reasoned that "If you don't throw that fastball when you have it, you can lose it." When he was traded to the Red Sox, however, he started to lose it, so he developed a curveball. It became an effective pitch, and after a dismal 8-8 season, Grove won twenty in 1935 and led the league in ERA four times between 1935 and 1940. Finally, in 1941 he won his dream 300th game, his last victory.

Mickey Mantle

One of the greatest baseball stories of all time is about "The Mick" facing daily his searing pain, and not only overcoming it, but becoming an all-time great in the face of it. Donald Honig said it most eloquently in *Baseball America*:

> *He awed his teammates with his power, his speed, and most of all with his grit. Injury prone throughout his career, he played on wobbly knees, with bandaged legs, with aching muscles. Playing through pain and excelling is one of the hallmarks of the great athlete, and some of them appear to take a primal satisfaction from it. It seems madness for them to do it, but at the same time it makes them seem dramatically summoned, elevating them to a yet higher dimension of fantasy, driving them even farther from the imaginative grasp of those who — sensibly — take to bed with a head cold. Teammates already impressed with such special talents were motivated and in some cases probably intimidated by what they saw; it gave a more sanctified glow to the aura of the Big Leagues. An injured god is a sobering sight; one who contends against the pain can be frightening.*

If his story weren't powerful enough, Mick's knee injury occurred during a dramatic moment involving the three best center fielders ever. It was in 1951, early in his career, during the World Series against the Giants. Mantle was in right field that day and tore out after a fly ball. He had it in his sights when he heard the great Joe DiMaggio call for it. Mantle slammed on the breaks just as his spike caught a drain cover, ripping up the knee. Who hit that fly ball? Willie Mays. Mick also had a shoulder operation, a broken foot and a torn ham-

Mickey Mantle

string. At one point fans could see blood through his pants from a hip abscess.

Mickey was born October 20, 1931, in a small house down a narrow dirt road in Spavinaw, Oklahoma. His dad, Elvin, known as Mutt, was a shoveler in a lead mine, a tenant farmer at times, and a semipro ballplayer. Mickey said his pop was good enough for the pros if he had ever been noticed. Mutt named Mickey after his favorite player, the great Mickey Cochrane. From the time Mickey was five, he and his dad played ball constantly, Mutt pitching, Mickey hitting, and brothers Roy and Ray shagging. Gramps would pitch lefty and Mutt righty to young Mickey, and this was the beginning of the greatest switch-hitter ever.

Mantle's career almost never happened. Mickey played football in high school and was seriously spiked in the shin as a sophomore. The leg festered until the local doctor recommended amputation, but Mutt and Mickey's mother, Lovell, drove him 175 miles to Oklahoma City where he got shots of a new wonder drug just released just that year. The drug was penicillin.

His long ball showed up early in youth and sandlot leagues. A Yankee scout, Tom Greenwade, scouting a teammate, saw The Mick switch-hit some of these awesome shots. On a rainy day following a game, the scout invited Mickey and Mutt into his Oldsmobile, and told them he would return after Mickey had finished high school and make him a Yankee. Greenwade did come back and signed Mickey to a Class D contract for a bonus of $1,150 and $140 per month.

Mickey was a shortstop at the time and made his share of errors plus some, but he batted .383 in 1950 with thirty-six homers, and earned a trip to the 1951 spring camp of the Yankees. No one had ever shown such power from both sides of the plate, and "The old perfesser" Casey Stengel took him under his wing. Phil Rizzuto owned the Yankee shortstop position, and Joe DiMaggio was still in charge of center field, so Mickey got a shot at right. He fizzled a bit and was sent down to the farm team for a month. Old Mutt, terminally ill, came for a visit, and put The Mick on course for good.

Mickey took over center field when Joe D. retired in 1952. Mantle punched out about twenty-five towering homers a season for several years, taking voracious cuts at the ball. In 1956 he had what is probably the best single season anyone has ever enjoyed in baseball, hitting .353 with fifty-two homers and 130 RBIs to win the Triple Crown. That same year, he missed being the only player to ever hit a ball *out* of Yankee Stadium by just eighteen inches. It was estimated to be a 600-foot shot (that's two football fields, folks!). One shot that cleared the Washington stadium was measured at 565 feet. Mantle played in twenty All-Star games, earned three MVP Awards, led his team to twelve World Series, and ended his career with 536 home runs.

Roger Clemens

R oger Clemens was born on August 4, 1962, in Dayton, Ohio, but the Clemens family moved to a suburb of Houston, Texas, when Roger was eight years old, after the death of his father. His childhood hero was Nolan Ryan, and from the earliest days, young Roger hoped to astonish observers with Ryan-like overpowering speed, exploding over the plate in a 95 mph fastball. He has achieved that, and unlike Ryan, Clemens coupled that speed with great control and a good curveball. It is that combination that places him among the best pitchers of all time.

Pitching at Spring Woods High School in Houston, Clemens was named to the all-state team. He did not yet have great speed, but threw hard with control. His local American Legion team won a state championship. Roger's 6'4", 200-pound-plus frame also enabled him to play football and basketball in high school.

The Twins drafted him in the twenty-second round after high school, but he opted to play for San Jacinto Junior College where he learned to finish his delivery strongly and developed his overpowering speed. He won All-America junior college honors in 1981.

Roger was a first-round draft pick by the Mets at that time, but opted to complete his education at the University of Texas, where he pitched the Longhorns' team to the College World Series Championship in 1983, twice being named an All-American.

In June of 1983, the Boston Red Sox drafted him in the first round (nineteenth pick overall). He ransacked Class A at Winter Haven and Class AA at New Britain, and won the East-

Roger Clemens

ern League Championship game. In 1984 he started AAA ball with Pawtucket, but was called up to Fenway Park in May. He was American League pitcher of the month in August with six straight victories, including a fifteen-strikeout game against Kansas City. An arm injury on August 31 forced him to end the season. In 1985 he got only fifteen starts. It was a season of pain for the rookie, and he underwent arthroscopic surgery in August.

The Red Sox coaches babied him along in the spring of 1986, unsure if he was ready to come back. Any questions about his shoulder were quickly answered as Roger pitched one of baseball history's most brilliant seasons. He won his first three games, and his nineteen strikeouts earned him the nickname "Rocket." Then on a cool evening in Fenway on April 29, he pitched his way into the record books and the Hall of Fame with an all-time record twenty strikeouts in one game, breaking the record of nineteen held by Steve Carlton, his hero Nolan Ryan and Tom Seaver. Clemens's fastball was clocked at speeds of 98 mph, and he struck out the side in the fourth and fifth innings, rolling up eight consecutive strikeouts. It was perhaps the most awesome performance in pitching history, and is regularly listed among the greatest games ever. Clemens went on to win his first fourteen games that year, the All-Star MVP, the Cy Young Award and the MVP. He faded a bit in postseason play, as the Red Sox lost the World Series in seven games.

A contract impasse caused him to miss spring training in 1987 and he got off to a slow start, but he finished up 20-9 and won his second consecutive Cy Young Award. He completed eighteen games that year, and also led the league in shutouts with seven. His 2.97 ERA came despite Fenway Park's toughness on pitchers—it is perhaps the best hitter's park in the majors—making The Rocket's feats even more amazing.

In 1988 Clemens set a Red Sox record with 291 strikeouts, led the league with eight shutouts, and won eighteen games. In 1990, he was second in Cy Young voting with a league-leading 1.93 ERA and a 21-6 record. He won his third Cy Young outright in 1991, again leading the league with a 2.62 ERA and 241 strikeouts. Roger's strikeout-to-walk ratio is an enormous 3:1, and his opponents' batting average is about .225, all in the best hitter's park around.

Roger was plagued a bit with temper problems, and was ejected from the fourth game of the 1990 AL championship series after arguing with an ump and using inappropriate language. He was fined $10,000 and suspended for five games. However, the Red Sox renewed his contract for a whopping $21.5 million over four years. I think he can pay the fine! The 1993 season found Roger in his first year-long slump, finishing 11-14 with a 4.46 ERA. The question is whether The Rocket will refind his location and continue his dominance over the major leagues.

Grover Cleveland "Pete" Alexander

I t was a cold day on February 26, 1887, in Elba, Nebraska, when Grover Cleveland Alexander was born. His father, William Alexander, was a farmer, and young "Pete" developed strong legs marching behind a plow in his early years. He was one of thirteen children, twelve boys, and he was named after the President of the United States. He played town ball in relative obscurity, working in a construction job for the local phone company and playing on Sundays. He played for the St. Paul team, and later for the Central City team, where he went 21-4 with a no-hitter. This went on until he was twenty-two, when he got a chance to play minor league ball.

Pete struggled somewhat in the minor leagues. He played for Galesburg in the Central Association of the Illinois/Missouri League, and in 1909 was struck in the head by a thrown ball while trying to break up a double play. He was unconscious for a few days, and subsequent double vision caused serious control problems. He was sold to the Syracuse Chiefs in the International League, where he picked up twenty-nine wins, including fifteen shutouts.

Finally, at the age of twenty-four, he was picked up by the Philadelphia Phillies where he was to spend the best seven years of his career. His rookie year was phenomenal. He won a league-leading twenty-eight games, and pitched thirty-one complete games and seven shutouts, allowing opponents a batting average of just .219. Despite pitching in Bakers Basin, where the right field wall was literally in his left pocket, a mere 272 feet away, Alexander led the league in wins four of seven years, led five times in strikeouts, and twice in ERA.

Grover C. Alexander

Alexander was an ungainly man, but on the mound his motion was graceful, smooth and economical: a little windup, a short stride, and a sweeping, three-quarter overhead delivery that made the ball seem to emerge from his chest. He rarely worked out or ran, warmed up quickly, wasted no motion or time, and got down to business. His games were quick, an hour and a half or so. He pitched fastballs and sharp curves, low and away, and was a master of control.

Hans Lobert played with Pete during those years, as reported by Lawrence Ritter in *The Glory of Their Times*. Lobert remembers Pete as a great big guy with a fine build, little short fingers, and a very heavy pitch, coming in like "a lump of lead." Lobert also remembers that Alexander was an epileptic, having seizures several times a season, although only on the bench, never on the mound. Many stories say he developed epilepsy during the war, but Lobert remembers it during the years with the Phillies from 1911 to 1918. Lobert said that the only thing that would stop the serious uncontrollable seizures was brandy, forced down Alexander's mouth, so they always had a bottle on the bench. Perhaps this is what led to Pete's alcoholism later in his career, since he never drank otherwise in his early years.

After three straight thirty-win seasons and three straight Triple Crowns (wins, strikeouts, ERA), Pete was called to military service just after the opening of the 1918 season. He saw plenty of bloody action and suffered partial deafness when a shell burst near his ear. He was traded to the Chicago Cubs while in service, and returned near the end of the 1919 season. He won twenty-seven games in 1920 with 173 strikeouts, a 1.72 ERA, and an unmatched record fourth Triple Crown for pitching.

In the final ten years of his career, Pete's alcoholism began to be quite apparent. He shrunk from reporters and became more of a solitary man, saying little, and then with a soft whispering voice. Although not as dominating as earlier, he still posted a 150-104 record during those years. He was known to pitch games fairly drunk, and usually had a few shots before a game.

It was during this time that his most famous game occurred. Due to Alexander's drinking, in mid-1926 Joe McCarthy traded him to St. Louis for the $6,000 waiver price, and Pete found himself in the World Series. He beat the Yankees in the second and again in the fifth game of the Series. After game six, knowing he wouldn't pitch again, he got quite drunk. In the seventh inning of game seven, Alexander was asleep in the bullpen. With a 3-2 lead, the Cardinal pitcher tired and loaded the bases with Yankees. With Tony Lazzeri at the plate and two out, manager Rogers Hornsby woke up Pete and asked if he could do the job. Bleary and tired, Pete almost slipped up and Lazzeri clouted a foul homer. Pete bore down and struck him out. He retired the side in the eighth and, with two out in the ninth, walked Ruth, who was caught stealing to end the game.

Alexander retired in 1930, and went with a rather demeaning sideshow that reenacted his famous strikeout of Lazzeri. The alcoholism was debilitating by that time, and Alexander died alone, penniless, in a rented room in 1950.

Mike Schmidt

Destiny favored seven-year-old Mike Schmidt one day in Dayton, Ohio, as he stood on a tree branch some thirty feet above his family's backyard. He grabbed an electric wire carrying 4,000 volts, and somehow was able to let go as he fell to the ground. His sneakers insulated him, so the charge had passed through his body and out his shins, leaving an egg-shaped scar. When I think of stories such as this, or of Mickey Mantle's near amputation, or Ted Williams's fiery landing during the war, I wonder how many even greater players were not so lucky.

Mike's family owned Jack's Drive-In, and Mike worked summers serving ice cream floats, steaks and shakes. Mike's dad was a good athlete, who might have played pro but for the war, and he fully supported Mike's athletic development.

At Fairview High School, Mike was star quarterback, shortstop and clean-up hitter, and an excellent basketball player. Cartilage problems, perhaps caused by the electric charge as a boy, ended his contact sport career. He batted just .179 his senior year at Dayton, with only one home run.

He enrolled at Ohio University, without an athletic scholarship and with a career in architecture in mind. His knees still troubled him, so he could not complete the freshman basketball season. He strengthened the knees with weights and went out for baseball. By his junior year he was named All-America.

Phillies scout Tony Lucadello had been watching Schmidt since high school, somehow knowing all the time of the great potential in Mike. Lucadello never tipped off other scouts

Mike Schmidt

about his find, and in 1971 begged the Phillies to sign Mike in the first round.

The Philadelphia Phillies drafted Schmidt behind Roy Thomas in 1971. Mike played minor league ball at Reading and at Eugene in the Pacific Coast League, showing some power. He was moved up in 1973, and after a month out with a shoulder injury, he went on to hit eighteen homers. But his 136 strikeouts and a .196 batting average placed a question mark on his ability to play big-league ball.

Manager Danny Ozark became like a father figure to Mike, and together they worked endlessly on Mike's swing. Ozark also taught patience and how to relax at the plate. Mike's own self-confidence paid off, and next year he hit .282, thirty-six homers, and 116 RBIs.

Mike stood at 6′2″, 198 pounds, and his red hair belied a pleasant, even-tempered personality—a good guy! However, he always set high standards for himself. Even as a college player he insisted his teammates throw the ball "around the horn" the right way, as the pro's did. Such intensity made him sometimes seem distant and moody. But it was what drove him to excel. He was criticized by the media, often just for saying the wrong thing at the wrong time, and was not a favorite with the fans, particularly during his slumps, until late in his career.

However, Mike is simply the best third baseman who ever lived. His 548 homers will never be equalled at the third sack. He won three MVPs and picked up ten Gold Gloves. He led the league eight times in home runs, seven times in assists, and six times in double plays. All around, the best ever at the hot corner!

Special Honorable Mention: Ty Cobb

He is not on the first team. But I need to find a way to honor the memory of one of the top players from baseball's first half. I do so here.

Unfortunately, I'm saddened by the facts that make up Ty Cobb's bio. Ty Cobb was the most disliked ballplayer of all time. Players who knew him cited his extreme sensitivity, and his need to be the best, as the roots of his problems with people, but these are the very factors that propelled him to the top of his game. He was troubled later in life by his image, and wrote in *My Life in Baseball: The True Record*, "I find little comfort in the popular picture of Cobb as a spike-slashing demon of the diamond with a wide streak of cruelty in his nature. The fights and feuds I was in have steadily been slanted to put me in the wrong."

Tyrus was born on December 18, 1886, in a post-Civil War farming community at Narrows, Georgia. His father was a schoolmaster, and the family was not poor. "We had status," wrote Cobb, "and upward of one hundred acres of tillable soil." However, speaking of a lady friend, "I was ashamed to have her see me in overalls doing farm labor," he wrote. "I was a Cobb and stuck behind a mule that broke wind when the breeze was the wrong way, and I resented it deeply."

At age fourteen he tried out with a "country baseball" team called the Royston Reds and soon began to earn himself a name. At seventeen he earned a tryout with Augusta in the newly formed South Atlantic Baseball League. His father argued with Ty well into the night about his desire to play ball, but finally agreed to let him get it out of his system, and wrote him six checks for $15 to help with expenses. Cobb did not

Ty Cobb

make the team, apparently (as reported by Fred Lieb) for not taking orders. But he landed a spot for $65 a month with Anniston in the semipro Southeastern League and led the league in batting. Augusta then reconsidered. Cobb won that league's batting lead, too, and was sold to the Detroit Tigers.

The course of baseball was about to change. Few players have had such an impact as to impress the game with a personal mark. Ty was often called the fastest thing in flannel, but he argued, "Discerning observers saw through my plan of attack . . . my speed was linked to a 'new style' of running bases, based on observation of pitchers, catchers, infielders and outfielders, the forcing of errors by doing the totally unexpected."

In an article for Christy Walsh's *Baseball's Greatest Lineup*, H.G. Salsinger of the *Detroit News* wrote about Cobb:

> *He was a fiery genius, brilliant and unorthodox. He dominated the game for more than two decades, changed infield and outfield play, lifted baseball out of the doldrums, revolutionized it, vitalized it.*
>
> *His is the story of a mighty brain and the driving force of genius that made him great when other men, superior in physical strength, natural ability and speed remained mediocre.*
>
> *His is the story of a tireless and burning ambition, a ceaseless effort to excel.*
>
> *Cobb became baseball's greatest player because he out-thought his rivals, kept a play ahead of them. His wide edge over the field was mental. He thought more quickly than the others and put his mechanical skill to better use than they did.*
>
> *There were players who could run as fast as Cobb, and a few who could run faster, but none ever matched him as a base runner. There were outfielders who could throw better than Cobb and players who could hit the ball farther, but they are not to be compared with him as fielders or hitters.*
>
> *In running bases, Cobb's lightning brain worked faster than his legs. He continuously crossed up fielders. He would break unexpectedly, then fail to break when they expected him to. Every move he made was carefully planned. Going into a base, he knew precisely how the infielders would try to make the play, and suited his own actions to the fielder's. He developed differ-*

ent slides, including the fadeaway, fall away and the hook. . . .

He constantly upset batteries and infields. He caused them to be overanxious and to overhurry. He was responsible for more wild throws than any player in history. He scored from first on singles, streaked from first to third or scored from second on infield outs, scored from second on outfield flies and sacrifice bunts.

Cobb ended his autobiography with, "When I played ball, I didn't play for fun. It's a contest, a struggle for supremacy, a survival of the fittest."

Too bad. He could have had the most fun of all.

PART FOUR

Doodads

The Dream Team
Manager

I didn't know whether to include this section. Picking the best manager for all time is like picking the best sports author . . . who cares? I never heard a heated debate about whether Billy Martin was a better manager than Earl Weaver.

Besides, I picked this team after a lot of work, so of course I figured I'd be the manager! Then reality set in. I began to worry about what would happen if the second-string team, a mighty good one, beat the first team in a seven-game series. Who would I have to blame? Who could I fire?

So I decided to take a shot at picking the best manager. Having done so, I'm convinced that the selection of the best manager ever cannot be objectively made. There is very little measurable about managers which is a result of their individual efforts. They depend very much upon the talent they have. Moreover, leadership on a team often comes from veteran players as much or more than from the manager. I do intend to make a choice, but I can't say I really sweated out the selection. Nonetheless, managers have become an important part of the game, and there is some interesting material about them.

As with everything else in baseball, managers are as different from each other as fish from fowl. Our review in the last chapter of the backgrounds of the great players showed them to be quite different personalities, and managers are no exception to the rule. Most great managers were exceptional judges of talent, and won by stocking teams and then sticking with potentially great players. Whitey Herzog managed the last place St. Louis Cardinals in 1980. He became general manager for a year, revamped 70 percent of the team, and made a series of great trades, acquiring the likes of Ozzie Smith, Bruce Sutter and Willie McGee. He then rode this team to the 1982 World Series.

In addition to knowing talent, some managers were street fighters, like Billy Martin and Earl Weaver, who knew the game and the rules better than most umps. They fought, argued, scrapped, and pushed their players to successful seasons. They were insistent on the game being played their way. John McGraw was the class of this genre, and was also a genius at devising innovative strategies to win.

Other managers were less visible, less confrontational with both players and umps. Bill McKechnie was even accused of being too gentle on his way to building great defensive teams. Connie Mack was a dignified gentleman who managed quietly and most patiently. He dressed in a suit with high, starched collars, even on the hottest of days, and moved his players around with a flick of his ever-present scorecard. He rarely argued with anyone, let alone umpires. He built and dismantled two dynasties during his fifty-three years of managing. Miller Huggins and Sparky Anderson were also great managers in the strong-but-silent-category, and it was largely Huggins who built the greatest team that ever played the game, the 1926-28 New York Yankees. Huggins had the two best hitters ever in Ruth and Gehrig, batting back to back. But Walter Alston, working without quite as much talent, accomplished more and was probably the class of this group.

My favorite type of manager falls in between street fighters and strong, silent guys. I don't want a fireball who burns out his players with an excess of passion, nor do I want a fellow who merely channels his players' energies. I have no problem with passion, or with inspiring it in others. But what is needed most is a manager who inspires teamwork, a leader who gets the whole team helping each other out. Casey Stengel, Frank Chance, Joe McCarthy, Al Lopez brought a more positive energy to the game, and, in my opinion, present a style more in keeping with the overall purposes of the game. They were not battlers, and took managing a level higher than the strong-but-silent group. They were leaders who unified teams in pursuit of the highest ideals of our American pastime.

Stein wrote a concise and very informative article on managing for the second edition of *Total Baseball*, and it's worth reading. Harvey Frommer's book *Baseball's Greatest Managers* affords an essay-level review of most of the best. Finally, there are full books on most of the greats. My main purpose here is to provide some stats and some insights. You can take it from there.

The following table lists the key statistics for the top twenty-five managers over baseball's history. The list of twenty-five includes managers nominated by various polls such as the *Players' Choice* survey, and Maury Allen's top 10 list. It also includes Hall of Fame managers, and those suggested by Stein and Frommer in their books. Two names missing which could have been here are Chuck Dressen and Hughie Jennings.

The managers are listed in chronological order. I identify only the teams they predominantly coached, and not teams they spent only a few years with (such as Dick Williams who coached in six cities, spending only three years in Boston, Oakland, California and Seattle). I have included the number of World Series (WS) wins, the number of Pennants (PEN), and the number of times their teams finished in the top two and the last two positions in the standings.

I have also included a statistic found in a number of record books known as A-E, or actual wins minus expected wins. This statistic is a creative attempt to see how well a manager could do in using the runs scored by his team over the runs scored by opponents. The idea is that a better manager will be able to channel the net offensive capacity of his team into more wins. The expected wins statistic looks like this:

$$\frac{\text{RUNS SCORED MINUS RUNS ALLOWED PLUS 81}}{\text{RUNS SCORED PER WIN}}$$

The opinion polls were as follows:

SPORTING NEWS CENTENNIAL	PLAYERS' CHOICE SURVEY	MAURY ALLEN'S PICKS	SPORTING NEWS MGR. OF THE YEAR
1. MCGRAW	1. STENGEL	1. STENGEL	MCCARTHY 3X
2. STENGEL	2. MCCARTHY	2. MCCARTHY	ALSTON 3X
3. MCCARTHY	3. ALSTON	3. MCGRAW	LARUSSA 3X
	4. MCGRAW	4. ALSTON	DUROCHER 3X

Casey Stengel was picked in the 1969 Centennial poll as the second-best manager in history. He was also number one in the players' survey, and first in Maury Allen's selection. It's hard to quarrel with that vote, considering what Stengel did with the Yankees during the prime of his managing career. He won .622 of games, ten pennants and seven World Series in twelve years. He was a towering leader, a molder of teams. But he also managed the Dodgers to eight losing seasons out of nine at the beginning of his managing career, and ended up with four straight last-place finishes with the expansion Mets. He would not be my choice.

John McGraw certainly towers over the game's first fifty years. He was a superb innovator, and had an uncanny ability to find raw talent and mold it (according to "his" way) into superstardom. He did so with Mathewson, Hubbell, Ott, Terry and others. Yet, I indicated earlier that the idea of the manager being the center of the team is not my choice approach. McGraw won only three of ten World Series, and none of his superstars are on my first team. I want a different kind of guy, a team guy who lets his athletes take the limelight as long as they do so as a team.

Alston is a tough one to pass up. He was a strong, silent type, but he also had too many problems with his stars. Jackie Robinson did not like him, and he had disputes with others too. Something is missing with him.

Joe McCarthy? He's my man! Holder of the best winning percentage among managers, he won seven World Series in nine tries, finished first or second seventeen times in twenty-four years, and never ended up in the second division. He won *The Sporting News* Manager of the Year award three times, and the paper didn't start giving it out until McCarthy had managed for ten years. The sabermetric (A-E) thing doesn't like him, but I do! Sure, he had some of the best talent ever, Ruth, Gehrig, DiMaggio. He was called the "push-button" manager. But he got these guys working together like no one ever. He was a master psychologist to handle a guy like Ruth with fewer problems than Miller Huggins had. He did the same for Hack Wilson, who did nothing before McCarthy got hold of him. He also got Rogers Hornsby off to his start. Sure, he inherited the

Joe McCarthy

wind, and he made of it the most efficient, fundamental, winningest team ever. He took a great team and kept it great, but that's the kind of team I'm giving him here. Harvey Frommer said, "Strictly business and stone jawed, Joe McCarthy was a master psychologist, an efficiency ex-

THE TWENTY-FIVE BEST SKIPPERS

PLAYER	CAREER	TEAM	WIN-LOSS	PCT	WS	PEN	TOP 2	LAST 2	YRS	A-E
Harry WRIGHT	1871-93	BOS/PHI	1,225-885	.581	NA	6	9	0	23	−39.7
Cap ANSON	1875-98	CHI	1,296-947	.578	NA	5	11	0	21	−3.2
Connie MACK	1894-50	PHI	3,731-3,948	.486	5	9	13	21	53	13.4
Fred CLARKE	1897-15	PIT	1,602-1,181	.576	1	4	9	1	19	−9.2
John MCGRAW	1899-32	NY	2,784-1,959	.587	3	10	21	3	33	−7.6
Clark GRIFFITH	1901-20	NY/WAS	1,491-1,367	.522	0	1	5	2	20	24.5
Wilbert ROBINSON	1902-31	BRO	1,399-1,398	.500	0	2	3	2	19	16.4
Frank CHANCE	1905-14, 23	CHI	946-648	.593	2	4	6	3	11	20.5
Miller HUGGINS	1913-29	STL/NY	1,413-1,134	.555	3	6	8	3	17	13.5
Bill MCKECHNIE	1915-46	BOS/CIN	1,896-1,723	.524	2	4	5	3	25	37.3
Bucky HARRIS	1924-56	WAS	2,157-2,218	.493	2	3	3	5	29	−32.5
Joe MCCARTHY	1926-50	NY	2,125-1,333	.613	7	9	17	0	24	−23.6
Casey STENGEL	1934-65	BOS/NY	1,905-1,842	.508	7	10	11	9	25	−4.8
Steve O'NEILL	1935-54	DET/PHI	1,040-821	.559	1	1	4	0	14	22.2
Walter DUROCHER	1939-73	BR/NY/CH	2,008-1,709	.540	1	3	10	2	24	−14.0
Al LOPEZ	1951-69	CLE/CHI	1,410-1,004	.584	0	2	12	1	17	28.3
Walter ALSTON	1954-76	LA	2,040-1,613	.558	4	7	15	0	23	36.8
Danny MURTAUGH	1957-76	PIT	1,115-950	.540	2	2	6	2	15	0.2
Dick WILLIAMS	1967-88	MON/SD	1,571-1,451	.520	2	3	5	5	21	7.0
Earl WEAVER	1968-86	BAL	1,480-1,060	.583	1	4	6	1	17	29.9
Billy MARTIN	1969-88	NY/OAK	1,253-1,013	.553	2	3	6	0	16	27.5
Sparky ANDERSON	1970-93	CIN/DET	2,069-1,750	.542	3	5	13	2	24	29.8
Whitey HERZOG	1973-90	KC/STL	1,281-1,125	.532	1	3	11	4	18	21.6
Tommy LASORDA	1976-93	LA	1,422-1,282	.526	2	4	6	1	18	−16.8
Tony LARUSSA	1979-93	CHI/OAK	1,202-1,033	.538	1	3	5	1	15	17.6

pert, and a man for whom rules and decorum paved the way for excellence. . . . His teams rarely beat themselves, he taught mental alertness."

Stengel is my second team manager. We'll have to see what he can do with Cobb!

The Baby Boomer Dream Team

S ome of my buddies have argued, successfully, that they can't relate to a Napoleon Lajoie or a Buck Ewing. They argue that competition is tougher now and ballplayers are better. All they care about is the players they have seen or who have played in their time.

We are the Baby Boomers, born in the post-World War II era, and so I'll suggest a team for that time. This team is limited to players whose careers started in 1950 or later. Most of these players were discussed while developing the All-Time Dream Team so I won't need to repeat all the analysis here. I'll just refer you to the appropriate section of the book.

OUTFIELD

Willie Mays, Mickey Mantle and Hank Aaron. Willie and Mickey are first team all-timers, so they clearly make this one! Hank edged out fellow Baby Boomer Frank Robinson in my earlier analysis, found in chapter five. Duke Snider would come in about fifth (although he started in 1947). Reggie Jackson, Frank Howard, Pedro Guerrero, Darryl Strawberry, Tim Raines, Dave Winfield and Roger Maris deserve mention. We'll keep an eye on youngsters like Barry Bonds, Jose Canseco, Kirby Puckett and Eric Davis. I'll let Frank Robinson DH.

FIRST BASE

This one is a bit tougher. The EBA statistic yields Dick Allen and Willie McCovey in the top twenty-five hitters list, with Willie Stargell, Harmon Killebrew, Norm Cash and Orlando Cepeda close behind among the top fifty or so batters. Stargell

Hank Aaron

Harmon Killebrew

actually played a bit more in outfield, but we remember him more at first base. Killebrew spent about a third of his time at third base. Keith Hernandez makes the list since he had the best glove in this era. He won twice the Gold Gloves of Don Mattingly, and had 20 percent more assists per game than Don, whose offensive contributions have now slipped below Keith's. Let's look at some numbers:

PLAYER	EBA % OVER LEAGUE	BR/A	HR	SB	DEFENSIVE LEVEL	MVP
ALLEN	142%	470	351	133	0 STAR	1 MVP
MCCOVEY	139%	538	521	26	0 STAR	1 MVP
STARGELL	133%	485	475	17	0 STAR	1 MVP
KILLEBREW	132%	500	573	19	1 STAR	1 MVP
CASH	127%	366	377	43	2 STAR	0 MVP
CEPEDA	126%	337	379	142	0 STAR	1 MVP
HERNANDEZ	120%	318	162	98	4 STAR	1 MVP

This is not an easy one; Allen was an all-time under-achiever, and had little defense. McCovey got an MVP but did not generally get many MVP votes, perhaps because he was overshadowed by Mays. Stargell and Killebrew did quite well in MVP voting generally. Cash was very good defensively, but was not a great player.

I'm going with Harmon Killebrew. His defense and MVP strength easily overcome Stargell. McCovey led the league in errors five times, and while we look for offense at first, we can't have a guy who can't catch at all! Hernandez had golden hands, but not quite enough stick for this primarily offensive position.

SECOND BASE

In chapter seven, Joe Morgan missed the all-time team by very little. He won't miss this team. Bobby Grich and Ryne Sandberg were somewhat better with the glove, but the defense presumption here is too slight to overcome Morgan's great lead in hitting. Rod Carew, Bill Mazerowski, Pete Rose and Lou Whitaker are a distant second.

Joe Morgan

Cal Ripken, Jr.

SHORTSTOP
I pretty clearly had Cal Ripken ahead of fellow baby boomer guys like Ernie Banks, Luis Aparicio, Robin Yount and Ozzie Smith. See the analysis in chapter eight, which included all of these players.

THIRD BASE
Mike Schmidt is first team all-time, and is well ahead of baby boomers Eddie Mathews, George Brett, Wade Boggs, Ron Santo, Chris Sabo and Terry Pendleton. No question here!

CATCHER
My earlier analysis dealt with Johnny Bench, Gary Carter and Carlton Fisk. Roy Campanella started in 1948. I find it much closer than most folks think between Bench and Carter. Although Bench got many more Gold Gloves, I feel Carter was better defensively. But Johnny Bench's two MVPs and superior batting put him ahead of the pack for the Baby Boomer's Team. The stats for these guys are in chapter ten.

PITCHERS
Thank God I get to pick four pitchers. My adjusted ERA analysis puts Roger Clemens, Sandy Koufax and Whitey Ford all on the team, in that order, as starters.

The last slot is a toss-up between Tom Seaver and Bob Gibson. Their stats are mighty close, both with an adjusted ERA 21 percent lower than the average of their time. Seaver had a better strikeout ratio and a much higher percent of wins above his team. He also dominated Cy Young voting more than Gibson did. Look at the stats in the pitcher section and make your choice. I'm starting Tom Seaver!

Here's the lineup and batting order for the Baby Boomer Team.

1. Joe Morgan 2B
2. Willie Mays CF
3. Mickey Mantle LF
4. Hank Aaron RF
5. Frank Robinson DH
6. Mike Schmidt 3B

Johnny Bench

Tom Seaver

7. Harmon Killebrew 1B
8. Johnny Bench C
9. Cal Ripken SS
P. Roger Clemens
   Sandy Koufax
   Whitey Ford
   Tom Seaver

The Modern Era Dream Team

The last set of complaints I got was from the generation below mine. They never saw Willie Mays or Mickey Mantle play, and wanted a dream team for the current era, guys they have seen.

I wanted to name the team, so I asked my twenty-four-year-old son what he called his generation, and he said, "The No Jobs Left" generation. But when I think about these ballplayers, I get the "Zillion Dollar Babies" team. In any event, you get the point. I thought I'd take a look at contemporary players. My idea was to get the players whose careers started in the last twenty years or so, the guys who, for the most part, are still active players. But, that's tough because there are so many coming out of the weeds now, and you just don't know who will make it. So I will look only at players with at least eight years in the majors through 1993.

OUTFIELD

Some of these players were not on my Top Fifty Hitters list because they played fewer than ten years, so I'll provide some stats for comparison. I won't go into great detail, but we'll take a reasonably close look at them. I cut off the list at 3-Star hitters, that is, players whose total offensive performance (adjusted EBA) was over 25 percent better than the average of their times. This left out guys like Jim Rice, Dale Murphy, George Foster, Dave Parker, George Bell, Dwight Evans, Fred Lynn, Tim Raines, Kirby Puckett and Tony Gwynn. The eight-year minimum rule left out Ken Griffey, Jr. (five years), but watch him! The twenty-year maximum rule cut out Reggie Jackson (1967), Amos Otis (1967) and Bobby Bonds (1968).

Rickey Henderson

Barry Bonds

PLAYER	EBA % OVER LEAGUE	BA	HR	SB	DEFENSIVE LEVEL	HONORS
R. HENDERSON (15 YRS.)	143%	.291	221	1,095	2 STARS	1 MVP
Barry BONDS (8 YRS.)	139%	.283	222	268	3 STARS	3 MVP
D. STRAWBERRY (10 YRS.)	137%	.259	290	205	0 STARS	RK. YR.
Eric DAVIS (10 YRS.)	130%	.262	196	299	2 STARS	
P. GUERRERO (15 YRS.)	127%	.302	215	97	1 STAR	
J. CANSECO (9 YRS.)	125%	.265	245	134	1 STAR	MVP RK. YR.
D. WINFIELD (20 YRS.)	125%	.285	453	220	2 STARS	

It's hard to compare guys with seven to eight years with vets of 15-plus years, but we'll let the numbers have their way in this. The outfield choice becomes pretty clear here. Henderson and Bonds are way out in front. I'd normally go with Davis over Strawberry for the defense, but Davis has been plagued with serious injuries, and it is not clear he will keep up. The trouble is that Strawberry is an incredible underachiever, and he also is on the decline. I think I'd rather give up a bit of offense and get Dave Winfield's glove on this team. Dave may even be a 3-Star fielder with that incredible arm of his; runners on first base would routinely hold up at second base on a single to Dave. So, the choices are Henderson, Bonds and Winfield. Strawberry can DH.

FIRST BASE

There are a slew of interesting guys on this list. Again, I cut off the selection at players whose earned bases average was 3-Star level, that is, about 125 percent better than league average. This eliminated Andres Galarraga, Paul Molitor, Glenn Davis, Alvin Davis, Mark Grace, Kent Hrbek and Don Mattingly. Mattingly's defensive excellence is not good enough to pull up his 116 percent EBA over league, which has declined with his cooled bat and lost power. Keith Hernandez, probably the best glove ever at first, started in 1974, but as we saw for the Baby Boomer team, he misses the cutoff with his 120 percent EBA over league. Those four defensive stars aren't enough at first base without more offense. Steve Garvey started in 1969, but only had a half dozen really good years anyway. John Olerud had only five years and Frank Thomas only four years in by 1993, but both will be on future lists if they stay healthy.

The defensive rating was based on assists per game, which for journeymen first sackers (five years' experience) averaged about .62 during the last fifteen years; errors per game (average .07); fielding percent; and Gold Glove recognition. 1 Star is average.

PLAYER	EBA % OVER LEAGUE	BA	HR	SB	DEFENSIVE LEVEL	HONORS
F. MCGRIFF (8 YRS.)	138%	.281	408	38	2 STARS	
M. MCGWIRE (8 YRS.)	133%	.249	229	6	2 STARS	RK. YR.
W. CLARK (8 YRS.)	125%	.299	176	52	2 STARS	
E. MURRAY (17 YRS.)	124%	.290	441	92	3 STARS	RK. YR.
C. FIELDER (8 YRS.)	123%	.259	191	–3	1 STAR	

It's hard to pass up Eddie Murray who has played his game consistently for sixteen years. But my rules here are for offense and Fred McGriff gets the nod on this team. First base is an offensive position.

SECOND BASE

The pickins' here seem mighty slim. Maybe I'm just spoiled by the all-around greatness of Lajoie, Collins, Morgan, and the wonder bat of Hornsby. These guys all had either great or at least above-average gloves, and had adjusted earned bases averages in the 550 range. See chapter seven.

In any event, I didn't include Rod Carew here. He started in 1967, and his 1-Star (average) defense wasn't good enough anyway. I also excluded players with low (below .450) EBAs like Steve Sax, whose glove is only a hair above average anyway. Frank White's glove (he won eight Gold ones) was above average, but his bat clearly wasn't. I also left out Harold Reynolds who somehow got three Gold Gloves with a pile of errors and hasn't much of a bat either. Roberto Alomar has just six years in the show, so he's not here for that reason. But we'll watch him closely after his MVP-class-year in 1993.

At second base we established that a player must be clearly

PLAYER	FA	PO/G	A/G	DP/G	DEFENSE LEVEL	EBA/A/N	HR	GOLD GLOVES
Ryne SANDBERG (13 YRS.)	.990	1.97	3.27	.59	3 STARS	.518/116%	240	9
Bobby GRICH (16 YRS.)	.984	2.39	3.05	.74	3 STARS	.522/116%	224	4
Willie RANDOLPH (19 YRS.)	.980	2.25	2.94	.72	2 STARS	.459/106%	54	0
Lou WHITAKER (16 YRS.)	.984	2.10	2.89	.67	2 STARS	.488/106%	218	3
AVERAGE (5-YR. PLAYERS)	.980	2.00	2.65	.59				

above average defensively to be eligible. After establishing that, we then see who could also hit.

Based on the above, it's pretty close between Ryne Sandberg and Bobby Grich. I analyzed the defense more closely in chapter seven and Sandberg came out ahead by a bit. He has a razor-thin lead in EBA, too. By a hair, I'll go with Ryne Sandberg.

SHORTSTOP

We had Cal Ripken as second to Honus Wagner on the all-time team, so he will clearly take his place on the field with this team of his contemporaries. Our rules required defensive excellence. Ripken is in the same class, though somewhat shy of Ozzie Smith, but well in front offensively. Robin Yount trails in both categories (see my analysis in chapter eight). I also looked at other Gold Glove shortstops (their Gold Gloves totals are in parentheses) who started since 1970, like Larry Bowa (2), Dave Conception (5), Roger Metzger (1), Rick Burleson (1), Alfredo Griffin (1), Tony Fernandez (4) and Ozzie Guillen (1). Yet, none of these players had EBAs above .460, so they are not even close.

Only Barry Larkin and Alan Trammel nibbled, as shown on page 216.

As I said earlier, there is no question about Ripken being the best this side of 1950.

THIRD BASE

Mike Schmidt! He and Eddie Mathews were the best-hitting third basemen ever, as analyzed before, and only Brooks Robinson (average bat) had a better glove.

Chris Sabo of the Reds has five years in and is a good future

PLAYER	FA	PO/G	A/G	DP/G	DEFENSE LEVEL	EBA/A/N	HR	GOLD GLOVES
Cal RIPKEN (13 YRS.)	.978	1.6	3.1	.68	4 STAR	.524/114%	297	2
Ozzie SMITH (16 YRS.)	.979	1.7	3.4	.63	4 STAR	.445/100%	23	13
Barry LARKIN (8 YRS.)	.972	1.6	3.1	.52	3 STAR	.508/113%	78	0
Alan TRAMMEL (17 YRS.)	.977	1.6	2.9	.62	3 STAR	.483/106%	174	4
Robin YOUNT (19 YRS.)	.964	1.7	3.2	.64	2 STAR	.498/108%	243	0

prospect. Edgar Martinez, in seven years with Seattle, is on fire, with a .343 BA in 1992. However, he is weak defensively and carries a .514 EBA in the Kingdome. Terry Pendleton came alive after his eighth-year free agency contract with the Braves; he had super years in '91 and '92 but has a long way to go before his .468 EBA can compete with Schmidt's monster .591 EBA. Bob Horner, a ten-year man with Atlanta, sported an adjusted EBA of .509. Defensive specialists Gary Gaetti, Buddy Bell and Tim Wallach all were below .500 EBA.

There is no one out there who will seriously threaten Schmidt's position. George Brett is second on this team with a .541 adjusted EBA and an above-average glove.

CATCHERS

Again, no need here for a lot of analysis. It was all done in chapter ten on catchers. Bench started in 1967, so he is not included here; Gary Carter started in 1972 and played until 1992. Carlton Fisk had a bat equal to Carter's, but Gary is one of the all-time greats defensively behind the plate.

Benito Santiago finished his seventh year in 1992 in San Diego, and is probably the best out there today with decent power, a .265 BA, and a great arm. Jim Sundberg, Lance Parrish, Bob Boone, Mickey Tettleton and Tony Pena all were below .500 EBA. Carter has the numbers, particularly the glove.

PITCHERS

We clearly determined that the best way to measure pitchers is by the earned run average (ERA). It's fairer to adjust it by the "park effect," and then compare this figure to the average ERA of the league during the player's career. For veterans with at least seven years in the majors who started since 1970,

Nolan Ryan

the adjusted ERA ranking is shown on page 218.

I looked at others, but their adjusted ERA was not far enough ahead of their times (Drabek 115 percent, Cone 114 percent, Viola 113 percent). No one else is close. Now, let's choose the starters!

Obviously Clemens! We placed him among the best of all time! I'll also stick with Saberhagen, particularly with that 3.38 strikeout-to-walk ratio and two Cy Youngs.

The next three are all pretty close, like the Cy Young winner, Hershiser. But he has never been the same since shoulder surgery in 1990. He is still great, but no longer is a 4-Star pitcher. Stieb and Tudor never got a Cy Young. But Greg Maddux has two of them, and was on fire in both 1992 and 1993. He makes the team! Nolan Ryan is down the list in adjusted ERA (112 percent), but he has seven no-hitters and the all-time lead in strike-

PLAYER	W	L	PCT.	SO	BB	ERA	PARK EFF.	ERA OVER LEAGUE	MVP	CY YOUNG
Roger CLEMENS (9 YRS.)	152-72		.679	1,873	552	2.80	114%	151%	1	3
Goose GOSSAGE (21 YRS.)	117-102		.534	1,433	691	2.93	95%	127%	0	0
Bret SABERHAGEN (9 YRS.)	113-83		.577	1,174	358	3.23	103%	126%	0	2
Orel HERSHISER (10 YRS.)	116-82		.586	1,230	539	2.87	88%	123%	0	1
Dave STIEB (14 YRS.)	174-132		.569	1,631	1,003	3.37	107%	123%	0	0
John TUDOR (12 YRS.)	117-72		.619	988	475	3.12	106%	123%	0	0
Dwight GOODEN (9 YRS.)	142-66		.683	1,686	575	2.99	94%	118%	0	1

outs. Opponents bat only .203 against him. I'll say he overcomes the presumption of the few ERA points he is down. So, it's Clemens, Saberhagan, Maddux and Ryan.

Goose Gossage was an intimidating, powerful reliever, but only a reliever, and I'm going only with starters. Besides, Gossage's winning percentage was only twelve points higher than his teams' over his career. But if I wanted a reliever, it would surely be him, even over Eckersley whose adjusted ERA is only 117 percent better than the league.

Here's the lineup and batting order for the Modern Era Dream Team.

1. Rickey Henderson LF
2. Dave Winfield RF
3. Barry Bonds CF
4. Fred McGriff 1B
5. Mike Schmidt 3B
6. Darryl Strawberry DH
7. Ryne Sandberg 2B
8. Cal Ripken SS
9. Gary Carter C
P. Roger Clemens
   Bret Saberhagen
   Orel Hershiser
   Nolan Ryan

Baseball's All-Time Dream Team: A Summary

J ust to recap, the following summarizes the All-Time Dream Team choice.

POSITION	FIRST TEAM	SECOND TEAM	HONORABLE MENTION
OUTFIELD	Babe RUTH	Joe DIMAGGIO	Rickey HENDERSON
	Willie MAYS	Tris SPEAKER	Frank ROBINSON
	Mickey MANTLE	Hank AARON	Pete ROSE
			Roberto CLEMENTE
DESIGNATED HITTER	Ted WILLIAMS	Ty COBB	
FIRST BASE	Lou GEHRIG	Jimmie FOXX	Stan MUSIAL
SECOND BASE	Nap LAJOIE	Eddie COLLINS	Rogers HORNSBY
			Jackie ROBINSON
			Joe MORGAN
SHORTSTOP	Honus WAGNER	Cal RIPKEN	
THIRD BASE	Mike SCHMIDT	Brooks ROBINSON	
CATCHER	Buck EWING	Bill DICKEY	Mickey COCHRANE
PITCHERS	Walter JOHNSON	Sandy KOUFAX	Steve CARLTON
	Lefty GROVE	Christy MATHEWSON	Nolan RYAN
	Roger CLEMENS	Cy YOUNG	
	Pete ALEXANDER	Carl HUBBELL	
		Satchel PAIGE	
MANAGER	Joe MCCARTHY	Casey STENGEL	

GLOSSARY

Abbreviations and Statistical Terms

A. Assists. An assist is recorded when a fielder does just that, "assists" in making an out. Typical assists occur when an infielder catches a grounder and throws the ball to first base for a force-out. The thrower gets an assist, and the first baseman gets a putout. Another example is when an outfielder catches a pop-up and throws to the catcher or another infielder who then tags out a runner. Here the outfielder gets a putout for the catch, and an assist for the throw. The infielder who makes the tag gets a putout. Thus, assists are primarily a good measure of throwing ability.

AB. At bats. The number of times a player comes to the plate to try to get on base. It does not include those times when a walk was issued, for some odd reason.

A/G. Assists per game. I prefer this statistic over merely counting the number of assists in a player's career, which depends on the number of games he played. Assists per game is a better measure of ability (as opposed to longevity). When this stat is further divided by the league's average number of assists per game, we obtain a measure of how much better a player was in this category than the average player. For shortstops and third basemen particularly, this is a most useful statistic.

BA. Batting average. The number of hits divided by the number of at bats. This is the most used measure of offensive performance over baseball's history. However, it is less important today since it counts all hits equally, and thus does not capture the greater value of the long ball. It also does not incorporate the value of walks or steals.

BB. Bases on balls, which are better known as walks. A free trip to first base as a penalty to the pitcher when he fails to get the ball over the plate four times in an at bat. In the earliest days, the batter was awarded first base but charged with an "out." It took nine bad pitches to get a base on balls in the early days (1876), with the number slowly reduced to today's four.

BR. Batting runs. Described in detail in chapter two. This sabermetric equation estimates the number of runs generated by a batter by counting weighted hits and subtracting weighted outs.

BR/A. Designates that the statistic has been adjusted by the park effect and compared to the league average.

CG. Complete games pitched.

CS. Caught stealing. Generally subtracted from steals to get at net steals.

Cy Young Award. Awarded to the most valuable pitcher each year by a group of writers, one from each major league city.

DP. Double plays. **DP/G** counts double plays per game, again a superior measure of defensive performance.

E. Error. Recorded against a player for failure to make a play which required only an average effort.

EBA. Earned bases average. This is the primary statistic developed for this book to measure offensive performance. It counts the number of bases earned for each plate appearance, divided by plate appearances. It is described in detail in chapter two. It is better than the slugging average since it not only counts extra base hits, but also incorporates walks and net steals. It is simpler than the estimated and weighted stats of contemporary statisticians, and thus has the virtue of understandability.

EBA/A/N. Signifies that the EBA has been adjusted for the park effect and compared to the league average; thus it provides a measure of how far a player was ahead of the average of his time.

ERA. Earned run average. This is the best measure of pitching performance over all of baseball's history, and is discussed in detail in chapter eleven. It is the primary statistic used here to pick the dream team pitchers. **EBA/A/N** signifies that the ERA has been adjusted for the park effect and compared to the league average. Thus it is a solid measure of how much better a pitcher was than the average of his time.

FA. Fielding average. Assists plus putouts divided by defensive chances (assists plus putouts plus errors). This is the primary measure of defensive ability over baseball's history. It is quite useless for catchers and first basemen, since they are credited with putouts for plays they have little to do with — strikeouts and force-outs respectively. Moreover, it does not sort out throwing ability (assists) and range (putouts) from surehandedness (errors).

FR. Fielding runs. Another complex estimated measure of runs saved by fielding. This one misses by a lot!

G. Games. The number of games played. A better measure is probably the number of innings played for purposes of stats like A/G, but the data is not publicly available at this time.

Gold Gloves. Awarded by *The Sporting News* to the best fielder at each defensive position.

H. Hits. Awarded when a runner safely reaches at least first base upon a batted ball, if no error is recorded.

HBP. Hit by pitch. A batter is awarded first base. I don't count it as "earned," and I understand it's debatable.

HR. Home runs. Fair ball hit over the fence. The grandest hits in all of baseball. Rarely, a homer is recorded for balls which stay inside the park, usually upon a freak carom away from the outfielder.

IP. Innings pitched.

MVP. Most Valuable Player Award. Awarded each year to the best player in each league by a vote of sportswriters.

N. Normalized. Dividing a stat against the league average to obtain a statistic, which then compares a player against the average of their times.

OAV. Opponents' batting average. A stat which measures the opponents' batting average against a pitcher.

OBP. On-base percentage. Hits plus walks plus HBP divided by plate appearances.

PA. Plate appearances. At bats plus walks.

Park Eff. Park effect. The extent to which the average runs scored is affected by the dimensions of a particular ballpark. Differences are often found in the amount of foul territory, the distances to the outfield fences, and climate conditions (wind, dampness). It is discussed in detail in chapter two. The factor is used to adjust offensive and pitching statistics.

PB. Passed ball. A failure of a catcher to catch a pitch which should have been caught, resulting in some advantage to the opposition.

Pct. Above Team. An interesting measure of the extent to which a pitcher's winning percentage is higher than the percentage of his team when the player was not pitching.

PO. Putouts. See **Assists**. Awarded when a caught ball or a tagged runner results directly in an out. A more useful measure is **PO/G** — putouts per game — which is a powerful performance measure, particularly of range and speed, when divided by the league average.

POS. Field position. 1B, First Base; 2B, Second Base; SS, Shortstop; 3B, Third Base; P, Pitcher; C, Catcher; RF, Right Field; CF, Center Field; LF, Left Field; U, Umpire.

PR. Pitching runs. A sabermetric estimate of the number of runs saved beyond what a league average pitcher might have saved. The formula for computing pitching runs is innings pitched × (League ERA/9) – earned runs allowed.

RBI. Runs batted in. Awarded to the batter when a runner scores upon a safely batted ball, a sacrifice or a walk.

Rk. Yr. Rookie of the Year. Awarded each year to the best rookie player in each league by the Baseball Writers Association of America.

SA. Slugging average. The number of bases earned by all singles, doubles, triples and homers, divided by at bats.

SB. Stolen bases.

SH. Shutouts. Completed games with no runs scored by one team.

SO. Strikeouts. See the discussion in chapter two on how the strike zone has changed over the years.

Star System. A rating system which classifies players into one of four levels, based on offensive or defensive performance.

3B. Three-base hits. Triples.

Trip Crwn. Triple Crown. Awarded to a batter who in a single year leads his league in batting average, runs batted in *and* home runs; and to a pitcher who in a single season leads the league in wins, ERA *and* strikeouts.

2B. Two-base hits. Doubles.

BIBLIOGRAPHY

Allen, Maury, *Baseball 100: A Personal Ranking of the Best Players In Baseball History*. Galahad Books, New York, 1981.

Davis, Mac, *100 Greatest Baseball Heroes*. True Books, Grosset & Dunlap, New York, 1974.

Faber, Charles F., *Baseball Ratings: The All-Time Best Players at Each Position*. McFarland & Co., Jefferson, North Carolina, 1985.

Farrell, James T., *My Baseball Diary*. A.S. Barnes & Co., 1957.

Frommer, Harvey, *Baseball's Greatest Managers*. Franklin Watts Pub., New York, 1985.

Graham, Frank, *The New York Giants*. Van Rees Publishing, New York, 1952.

Honig, Donald, *Baseball America*. Macmillan & Co:, New York, 1985.

Honig, Donald, *Baseball When the Grass Was Real*. Coward, McCann and Geoghegan, Inc., New York, 1975.

James, Bill, *The Bill James Historical Baseball Abstract*. Villard Books, New York, 1988.

Koufax, Sandy, with Ed Linn, *Koufax*. Viking Press, New York, 1966.

Langford, Walter M., *Legends of Baseball*. Diamond Communications Inc., Indiana, 1987.

Lieb, Fred, *Baseball As I Have Known It*. Coward, McCann and Geoghegan, Inc., New York, 1977.

Mantle, Mickey, with Herb Gluck, *The Mick*. Doubleday, New York, 1985.

Mays, Willie, with Lou Sahadi, *Say Hey*. Simon & Schuster, New York, 1988.

McCaffrey, Eugene and Roger, *Players' Choice*. Facts on File Publications, New York, 1987.

Neft, David S., et al., *The Sports Encyclopedia: Baseball*. St. Martin's, New York, 1990.

Newcombe, Jack, *The Fireballers*. Putnam, New York, 1964.

Peary, Danny, *Baseball Players*. Simon & Schuster Inc., New York, 1990.

Reichler, Joseph L., *The Baseball Encyclopedia*. Macmillan Publishing Company, New York, 1985. Also, ninth ed. 1993.

Riley, James A., *The All-Time All-Stars of Black Baseball*. TK Publishers, New York, 1983.

Ritter, Lawrence, *The Glory of Their Times*. Random House, New York, 1985.

Ryan, Nolan, with Harvey Frommer, *Throwing Heat, the Autobiography of Nolan Ryan*. Avon Books, New York, 1988.

Schmidt, Mike, *Always on the Offense*. Atheneum, New York, 1982.

Seymour, Harold, *Baseball, the Early Years*. Oxford University Press, New York, 1960.

Shatzkin, Mike, and Jim Charlton, *The Ballplayers*. Arbor House/William Morrow, New York, 1990.

Thorn, John, ed., *The Armchair Book of Baseball*. Charles Scribner's Sons, New York, 1985.

Thorn, John, and Palmer, Pete, eds., with David Reuther, *Total Baseball*. Warner Books, New York, 1991.

Turkin, Hy, *The 1955 Baseball Almanac*. A.S. Barnes and Company Inc., New York, 1955.

Walsh, Christy, *Baseball's Greatest Lineup*. A.S. Barnes and Company, Inc., New York, 1952.

Williams, Ted, as told to John Underwood, *My Turn at Bat*. Simon & Schuster, New York, 1969.

INDEX